Swanson on Internal Auditing

'Raising the Bar'

Swanson on Internal Auditing

'Raising the Bar'

DAN SWANSON

IT Governance Publishing

IT Governance Publishing
IT Governance Limited
Unit 3, Clive Court
Bartholomew's Walk
Cambridgeshire Business Park
Ely
Cambridgeshire
CB7 4EH
United Kingdom

www.itgovernance.co.uk

First published in the United Kingdom in 2010
by IT Governance Publishing.

ISBN 978-1-84928-067-9

WHAT OTHERS ARE SAYING ABOUT THIS BOOK

In Dan Swanson's hands ... internal audit becomes the lantern of Diogenes, illuminating accountability, responsibility and control.

Jon Lukomnik, Sinclair Capital LLC

Internal auditing and information security are inextricably intertwined. Dan Swanson is highly qualified to write on the first and uniquely credentialed to write on the second. ... He is truly a phenomenon in the field and this book shows it.

Alexandra R Lajoux, Chief Knowledge Officer
National Association of Corporate Directors

Swanson on Internal Auditing: Raising the Bar will serve as a guide for auditors, both new and old, in navigating the changing landscape in which professionals function!

Jim Kaplan, CIA, CFE, President and Founder of AuditNet.org,
the Global Resource for Auditors

Raising the Bar is a new ready reference for the audit professional. ... The book is a helpful reference for all auditors and it professionals.

Brian Barnier, ValueBridge Advisors

This book deserves its place in the audit library and is a recommended resource for all internal audit professionals.

KH Spencer Pickett

What Others Are Saying About This Book

Dan Swanson has carved out a special niche in internal audit cyberspace. ... He is the epitome of the Institute of Internal Auditors' driving force – *"progress through sharing"*. At last Dan has brought his unrivalled, unique experience to bear ...

Professor Andrew Chambers

Dan's new book covers a wealth of material and is not restricted to his specialized fields of IT auditing and information systems security ... he provides concise commentary on strategic issues regarding the way internal audit is established, planned and performed.

Scott Mitchell, CEO, OCEG

Internal audit is facing the new challenges of a new world. ... Swanson shows how organizations can best use the audit function as a strategic tool and how audit professionals can rise to the opportunity. You ignore Swanson's message at your peril.

Rick Telberg, Editor/Publisher, CPA Trendlines

Regardless where you are in your internal audit career, you can benefit from Dan's efforts and the resources within this book. Keep this book handy, it will serve you and your work efforts very well.

Dan Ramey, CPA, CIA, CFE, CFF, CISA, Audit Director
Pannell Kerr Forster of Texas PC – Houston

Dan shares with us a wealth of knowledge in these pages with marvelous nuggets of wisdom on every page. Enjoy!

Dr Gary Hinson, PhD, MBA, CISA, CISM, CISSP

FOREWORD

Asking questions is a very good way to find out about something.

Kermit the Frog

Wise advice, even in this day of high-tech business, and even if attributable to Kermit the Frog!

They say that a good reporter knows a little about everything, and a lot about nothing. I've always believed in the wisdom of that statement through all my years as a reporter covering local government, crime, politics, science, and human interest – but not until I started writing about corporate governance did I fully appreciate how well that saying applies to business professions as well. Perhaps it fits best of all to the internal auditor.

In the seven years that I have written about corporate governance, I've developed a certain fondness for the internal auditor. He (or she) roams the company corridors, inspecting projects in various other departments to see that they pass muster. He enters the room with a critical eye, asking questions that try to be polite, but nevertheless are often unwanted. The internal auditor fights a constant battle for more resources and more respect; everyone says the internal auditing function is important, but when the time comes to approve budgets or grant access to important sources of information – well, not so much. (That, too, sounds quite familiar to us in the news business.)

I've also watched corporations struggle with internal auditing conceptually: Do we really need an internal audit function at my company? What is an internal auditor supposed to do? Who supervises him? Who sets the criteria he uses to judge our operations as effective or compliant? What happens when he decides something isn't effective or compliant? Where does this person fit on the organizational chart? How many staff does he need? What do we pay him?

Here, in one straightforward volume, Dan Swanson answers those questions, and gives companies the practical advice they need to put their internal-auditing function to work.

That guidance is still sorely needed. Yes, corporate governance as a whole, and internal auditing specifically, did receive a giant boost in awareness with the passage of the Sarbanes-Oxley Act in 2002: the landmark, exacting law mandating that publicly traded companies produce reliable financial statements. However, for most of the intervening years since then, corporations have perceived internal auditing only in terms of SOX compliance – whatever you had to do to meet the letter of the Sarbanes-Oxley law, you did; that qualified as the company's internal audit function or (even better) "doing corporate governance." Anything beyond that was unnecessary, and could be postponed or discarded.

For a brief period in the middle of the 2000s, corporations could get away with that narrow view. Internal auditors – and their CEO bosses, and their boards of directors – devoted all their time to the minutiae of internal controls, accounting procedures, and segregation of duties that comprise compliance with SOX. It was a wholly new experience for many companies, and it consumed them. Other elements of a strong internal audit function could be ignored simply because internal audit teams had no time to do anything else anyway.

Two things happened to bring that era to a close. First, companies learned how to cope with SOX compliance and bring its exhaustive requirements under control. Then, the financial crisis of 2008 arrived, reminding us that companies were still bad at plenty else.

Contrary to what some cynics say, the financial crisis was not proof that SOX compliance is worthless. SOX was passed to ensure the accuracy of financial reporting, and with a very few questionable exceptions, none of the culprits in the financial crisis experienced reporting failures. They experienced risk management failures. The difference is huge. Nobody, in the lead up to the crisis, was telling investors, "We have $1 million in revenue" when in fact they had only $500,000. They were telling investors, "We have a portfolio of bonds we can sell for $1 million" that they could only sell for $500,000 when they tried to sell it.

Why didn't those companies know the portfolio was worth less? Why didn't they plan scenarios with lower figures? Why did they buy $1 million worth of bonds in the first place? Those are the questions that boards and senior managements never asked, and those are the "polite but nevertheless unwanted" questions I mentioned earlier, that internal auditors must ask in the future. They are questions that challenge assumptions, envision unlikely outcomes, and stimulate stronger thinking. From today forward, the internal auditor must play that role, of skeptical counselor, to help companies navigate the often-perilous world of risks that confronts them. We ignored that function in the 2000s, and look where it brought us.

Swanson's book can serve as a roadmap to develop that true internal audit function. He opens with chapters that explain the internal audit function as a concept, and then marches through one specific topic after another that internal auditors must know: risk management, IT security, business continuity, ethics and compliance, and much more. Many of the subjects in this book he first discussed in *Compliance Week*, and it has been rewarding to re-read them all here in one volume. Use this book as a reference manual to help frame the problems you face and guide the solutions you implement – because the importance of internal auditing is here to stay, and the profession is now complex and critical enough that you need all the help you can get.

Matt Kelly

Editor in Chief, *Compliance Week*

PREFACE

Dan Swanson is a seasoned internal audit professional who is well known in the field of internal auditing, governance, compliance and risk management. For many years, Dan has spearheaded drives to share and debate new developments that affect the work of the internal audit professional. Dan's new book provides a compilation of articles that he has prepared over the years, many of which have been published in *Compliance Week*, brought together in this important new knowledge portal. The challenges for internal auditing are real.

As an international profession, internal audit sits somewhere between assuming a low profile that barely raises a mention in governance regulations – through to being seen as a key solution to better corporate transparency in the way risk is perceived and addressed by large companies, government agencies and not-for-profit sectors. A low-key approach raises the danger of being overlooked and de-prioritized, while a higher profile creates great expectations which must then be fully met as auditors reach out towards a new, more challenging role. It is here that Dan's book comes into its own, in helping to identify the key issues that need to be part of the strategic re-positioning by chief audit executives who are demanding a seat at the governance table.

Preface

Dan's new book covers a wealth of areas and is not restricted to his specialized fields of IT auditing and information systems security, as he provides concise commentary on strategic issues regarding the way internal audit is established, planned and performed and also quality assured.

High-level issues sit alongside practical guidance to ensure the book has an appeal to all levels of internal audit management and staff, as each reader can dip into a range of different topics. In this way, the book provides much "what-to-do" conceptual guidance, as well as many "how-to-do-it" auditing pointers. That said, Dan clearly demonstrates his specialist knowledge of auditing information systems and this topic has to be one of the top 10 risks that most corporate boards have on their current agendas. Another feature of the new book is the way it employs Dan's ability to draw on a wide range of sources of information and knowledge. There are many references made to websites and significant documents that act as a roadmap to encourage further exploration. You will be able to dip into Dan Swanson's commentaries on the wide variety of topics that he has examined over the years, and then follow up the various references, including the most important work of the Institute of Internal Auditors.

This new book deserves its place in the audit library and is a recommended resource for all internal audit professionals.

KH Spencer Pickett

ABOUT THE AUTHOR

Dan Swanson is a 26-year internal audit veteran, who was formerly the Director of Professional Practices at the Institute of Internal Auditors.

Swanson has completed audit projects for over 30 different organizations, spending almost 10 years in government auditing (federal, provincial and municipal levels), and the rest in the private sector, mainly in the financial services, transportation and health sectors. Dan has completed more than 50 IT conversion audits and a dozen comprehensive audits of the IT function. He is currently focused on improving the practice of information security.

Swanson writes a monthly internal audit column for AuditNet, a bi-monthly IT audit column for the Association of Healthcare Internal Auditors (AHIA), and a monthly IT governance resource newsletter for IT Governance Ltd.

He previously wrote a monthly internal audit column for *Compliance Week*. He is the Managing Editor for *EDPACS*, a senior audit and control publication dedicated to improving the practice of IT audit and IT security. He has also written for numerous other organizations, including: ACCA (the Association of Chartered Certified Accountants), the American Bar Association (ABA), CIO Canada, IT Compliance Institute (ITCI) and KPMG's Audit Committee Institute (ACI). He contributes regularly to an information security blog for IT World Canada (ITWC). The author of more than 150 articles on internal auditing, information security and other management practices, Dan is currently a freelance writer by night and an information security officer for a large healthcare organization by day.

ACKNOWLEDGEMENTS

Over the years I've had the pleasure and opportunity to work with, and learn from, many senior practitioners and thought leaders in governance, risk management, IT and IT security, and IT and internal audit. I'd like to thank the following colleagues who have made a difference in my professional life:

- Allen, Julia: Software Engineering Institute, Carnegie Mellon University
- Anderson, Doug: Dow Chemical Company
- Barnier, Brian: ValueBridge Advisors
- Basham, Robin: Phoenix Business & Systems Process, Inc.
- Besko, Geoff: Seccuris, Inc.
- Bishop, Bill (deceased): The Institute of Internal Auditors
- Bloxham, Eleanor: The Value Alliance and Corporate Governance Alliance
- Brewer, Cass: Truth to Power (T2P)
- Brown, David: Brown Governance, Inc.
- Calder, Alan: IT Governance Ltd.
- Chambers, Andrew: Management Audit LLP
- Chambers, Richard: The Institute of Internal Auditors
- Chin, Angelina: General Motors Corporation
- Craven, Gary: PCGI
- Dawe, Gigi: The Canadian Institute of Chartered Accountants (CICA)
- Gazzaway, Trent: Grant Thornton LLP
- Gislason, Paul: Manitoba eHealth

Acknowledgements

- Goldmann, Peter: White-Collar Crime Fighter (Editor and Publisher)
- Halliday, Myles: Manitoba eHealth
- Hancox, David: Office of the New York State Comptroller
- Harrington, Larry: Raytheon Company
- Hines, Michael S: Administrative Business Consultants, Inc.
- Hinson, Gary: NoticeBored
- Jameson, Steven: Community Trust Bank
- Johnston, Craig: Investors Group, Inc.
- Jonas, Keith, Trusted by Design, Inc.
- Kabay, Mich: Norwich University, Northfield VT, USA
- Kaplan, Jim: AuditNet
- Kelly, Matt: Compliance Week
- Kim, Gene: Tripwire, Inc.
- Kral, Ron : Candela Solutions LLC
- Kreitner, Clint: Center for Internet Security (CIS)
- Lapointe-Young, Carman: CIA, CCSA, CFE, under-secretary-general for Internal Oversight Services (OIOS), United Nations
- Larkin, Gary P: KPMG Audit Committee Institute (ACI) and US Conference Board
- Lajoux, Alex: National Association of Corporate Directors (NACD)
- Legary, Michael: Seccuris, Inc.
- LeGrand, Charles: Managing Principal, TechPar Group, and CEO, CHL Global Associates
- Leech, Tim: Leech & Co GRC, Inc.
- Lopuck, William: Manitoba Department of Finance
- Lovell, Brenda: AACSB International
- Lukomnik, Jon: Sinclair Capital LLC.
- Leech, Tim: Leech & Co GRC, Inc.

Acknowledgements

- Malmquist, Warren: Molson Coors Brewing Company
- Marks, Norman: SAP
- McDaniel, Roger: Audit Services
- Mitchell, Scott: Open Compliance & Ethics Group (OCEG)
- Moxey, Paul: Association of Chartered Certified Accountants (ACCA)
- Northcutt, Stephen: The SANS Institute
- Parker, Donn: Retired
- Pickett, Spencer: National School of Government
- Power, Michael: Centre for Analysis of Risk And Regulation, London School of Economics (LSE)
- Ramamoorti, Dr Sridhar: Kennesaw State University
- Rasmussen, Michael: Corporate Integrity, LLC
- Roth, James: AuditTrends
- Schwartz, Malcolm: CRS Associates, LLC
- Seward, Jack: Jack Seward & Associates, LLC
- Shankar, N G: Aditya Birla Group
- Snell, Doug: Manitoba eHealth
- Sobel, Paul: Mirant Corporation
- Spafford, George: Spafford Global Consulting, Inc.
- Sparks, Don: Audimation Services and Caseware IDEA, Inc.
- Switzer, Carole, Esq: Open Compliance & Ethics Group

I particularly want to thank Charles LeGrand, Norman Marks and Gary Hinson who have each supported and helped guide my professional efforts over the years. Their insight and leadership has been inspirational in many ways, and their feedback has been invaluable in assisting me in all of my writings. I also want to thank my various editors and publishers, including: Cass Brewer, Alan Calder, Jim Kaplan, Gene Kim, Matt Kelly, Scott Mitchell and Dave

Acknowledgements

Webb. Finally, I must also thank Matt Kelly, Editor in Chief of *Compliance Week*, for his support and encouragement. The core foundation of this book is based on the monthly columns originally published by *Compliance Week* and with their permission are reproduced in their entirety here. We spent countless hours in discussion regarding the presentation and articulation of various audit issues, and this book was made possible because of that.

CONTENTS

Contents

Contents

Contents

Contents

Contents

BOOK OVERVIEW

It is not enough to do your best: you must know what to do and THEN do your best.

W. Edwards Deming

Raising the Bar provides a fascinating insight into the key issues facing the internal auditor. The author, Dan Swanson, is a seasoned internal audit professional who is well known in the field of internal auditing, governance, compliance and risk management. For many years, he has spearheaded drives to share and debate new developments that affect the work of the internal audit professional. This new book encompasses a compilation of articles that Dan has prepared over the years, many of which have been published in *Compliance Week*, brought together in this important new knowledge portal.

The challenges for internal auditing are real. As a profession, internal audit sits somewhere between assuming a low profile that barely raises a mention in governance regulations – through to being seen as a key solution to better corporate transparency in the way risk is perceived and addressed by large companies, government agencies and not-for-profit sectors. A low-key approach raises the danger of being overlooked and de-prioritized, while a higher profile creates great expectations which must then be fully met as auditors reach out towards a new, more challenging role. It is here that Dan's book comes into its own; in helping to identify the key issues that need to be part of the strategic re-positioning by chief audit executives who are demanding a seat at the governance table.

Part 1 covers the professional practice of internal auditing. Chapter 1 provides an introduction to internal auditing and includes guidance on setting up an internal audit function, from "step zero" using a suitable executive sponsor. The fact that internal-audit efforts must be risk based and contribute to the long-term assurance needs of the organization and its board is made clear and an outline of the top 12 internal audit priorities is used to assist the development of long-term audit plans. Moreover, the value added from internal audit is set against the importance of preserving the integrity and independence of audits, as the internal auditor seeks to maintain a delicate balance between offering advice (mainly consulting services) and providing opinions about a process, system, account balances, or other subject matter (assurance services).

Chapter 2 develops some of the themes from Chapter 1 and deals with improving internal-audit results. Quality internal auditing is seen as the main way of achieving better results, drawing on the Institute for Internal Auditors *International Standards for the Professional Practice of Internal Auditing*. This chapter also covers the important art of expressing an internal-audit opinion using an appropriate control model that is driven by an assessment of risks across the organization. The chapter also explains how the all-important audit universe can be used to address the potential risks facing the organization in line with internal auditing's unique position within a company, as it provides management and audit committee members with valuable assistance, by giving an objective assurance on governance, risk management and control processes.

Chapter 3 deals with the professional practice of internal auditing and highlights how, as one of the cornerstones of corporate governance (along with the Board of Directors, senior management and external auditing), internal auditing can provide strategic, operational and tactical value to an organization's operations. The chapter also addresses the impact of internal auditing on important areas, such as reviewing the effectiveness of the finance department and critical IT investment decisions by management and the Board, as well as the wider topic of board oversight of IT. There is more practical advice on topics such as auditing ethics and compliance programs bearing in mind that compliance can be a daunting challenge, but it is also an opportunity to establish and promote operational effectiveness throughout the entire organization. Chapter 3 would not be complete without a mention of fraud, and audit's role in detecting and preventing fraud is discussed along with the need for organizations to be ever diligent when developing a robust anti-fraud program.

Dan's new book covers a wealth of material and is not restricted to his specialized fields of IT auditing and information systems security, as he provides concise commentary on strategic issues regarding the way internal audit is established, planned and performed and also quality assured. High-level issues sit alongside practical guidance to ensure the book has an appeal to all levels of internal audit management and staff, as each reader can dip into a range of different topics. In this way, the book provides much "what-to-do" conceptual guidance as well as many "how-to-do-it" auditing pointers. That said, Dan clearly demonstrates his specialist knowledge of auditing information systems and this topic has to be one of the top 10 risks that most corporate boards have on their current agendas.

Chapter 4 notes some of Dan's favorite websites and resources that the reader can explore further, while Chapter

5 covers IIA related guidance, including the International Professional Practices Framework (IPPF) and further guidance for internal audit professionals.

Chapter 6 deals with priorities for the coming decade and goes into some detail on four key areas:

- auditing the ERM program
- protecting digital assets
- operational resilience
- corporate governance.

The crucial concept of "internal audit's seat at the governance table" is dealt with, spurred on by the Institute of Internal Auditors advocating that internal audit should be one of the cornerstones of good governance.

Part 2 covers the practice of IT auditing, while Chapter 7 covers IT audit and discusses the significant opportunity for internal audit to deliver real value to the Board and executive management. There is much practical guidance on auditing various aspects of IT, including:

- major IT initiatives
- company IT strategies
- technology changes
- technology change processes
- information security
- privacy programs
- records management
- business continuity programs.

Dan draws on his specialist knowledge of IT auditing and IT security for Chapter 8 using his IT column for the Association of Healthcare Internal Auditors (AHIA) in their internal audit publication entitled *New Perspectives*. The focus is on ensuring both IT and the business is properly aligned.

Chapter 9 goes further into the world of IT governance and details various IT audit checklists covering:

- information security
- change management
- IT governance and strategy
- privacy and data protection
- risk management.

Chapter 10 delves into Dan's column for AuditNet® and the many website references that underpin the audit and information security reviews that ensure corporate resources are protected. There is some mention of corporate risk management and the need to carry out a comprehensive review of corporate risk management practices and governance arrangements. IT governance is given some exposure in line with the view that data privacy may well be the next big organizational challenge. Even as information privacy and protection objectives grow more critical and complex, they are also increasingly subject to scrutiny by both internal and external auditors. One feature of Chapter 10 is the "summer reading" that Dan recommends covering an interesting array of topics. Chapter 11 gives reference to Dan's numerous resource blogs from the IT World Canada website, while Chapter 12 covers *Sentinel*: the IT Governance monthly newsletter. Chapter 13 dips into the CIO Canada IT Management columns that provide the leading IT management resources used by CIOs and senior IT managers. The final chapter of Part 2, Chapter 14 is an interesting collection of risk management based material dealing with the much overlooked task of "keeping our kids safe" in an online world.

Dan completes his book with Part 3, Chapter 15 by emphasizing the importance of continuous improvement and highlighting an article about Dr Deming. He includes his three favorite business books, 1) *The goal: a process of ongoing improvement*, 2) *Crucial conversations: tools for talking with stakes are high* and 3) *Crucial confrontations: Tools for Resolving Broken Promises, Violated Expectations, and Bad Behavior* (2005). There are various appendices in this new book covering a variety of topics including:

- a comprehensive *EDPACS* article on IT auditing (Dan is the managing editor for the *EDPACS* publication)
- a primer on corporate duties – taken from the OCEG *Internal Audit Guide*.

As is clear, there is much made of Dan's ability to draw on a wide range of sources of information and knowledge. There are many references made to relevant websites and significant documents that act as a roadmap to encourage further exploration. You will be able to dip into Dan Swanson's commentaries on the wide variety of topics that he has examined over the years, and then follow up the various references, including the most important work of the Institute of Internal Auditors.

This new book deserves its place in the audit library and is a recommended resource for all internal audit professionals.

KH Spencer Pickett, MSc, FCCA, MIIA, FIIA, CFE

INTRODUCTION

Quality is not a sprint; it is a long-distance event.

Daniel Hunt

Whether you are new to internal auditing or an experienced practitioner or academic, there will be something for you in *Raising the Bar*. Dan Swanson's collection of insights covers a diverse collection of management subjects and governance issues.

I am pleased to see Dan include some of my work, notably a reference to the "State of Internal Auditing" that was published in *EDPACS* in 2009. Probably with that in mind, I am honored that he asked that I contribute my views concerning the future of our profession.

This is indeed a critical time for internal auditing. Fortunately, leadership at the Institute of Internal Auditors (IIA) and among prominent practitioners has recognized the need for change. The 2010 General Audit Management (GAM) International Conference saw a number of IIA and other eminent thought leaders confront the needs head on.

My friend Richard Anderson, a major contributor to the risk management profession over the years and a former partner with PricewaterhouseCoopers in the UK, wondered at the international conference whether internal auditing had become irrelevant. As he pointed out, few, if any, held internal auditors to blame for any aspect of the great recession. Although there is a widely held view that corporate governance and risk management practices failed, nobody has said "where were the internal auditors?"

I join in the refrain: "where are the internal auditors?" If we are to be relevant, chief audit executives (CAEs) have to refocus on providing assurance regarding how well management identifies, evaluates, responds and manages risks – including the controls that keep risk levels within organizational tolerances.

That means that:

- The audit plan has to be designed to address the major risks to the enterprise. The traditional risk-assessment process must die a quick death (assessing risk levels based on an audit universe, and then performing audits of the controls designed to address risks to the achievement of objectives for those areas, locations, business units, etc.) A top-down risk assessment process will take its stead. Here the more significant risks to the enterprise are identified and targeted in audit engagements. Rather than focus on risks to objectives at a process, department or location, audits will focus on risks to the objectives of the organization.
- Every audit report should include an opinion on the overall management of the risks under review and the adequacy of related controls. I fail to understand how internal auditors believe they provide assurance (required by the IIA Standards) when they don't provide an opinion (which is not, for some reason, required by the Standards). I also fail to understand how audit committees and top management suffer CAE fools who are reluctant to give an assessment.
- The audit plan should be designed to provide assurance on the major risks, not just perform audits. In other words, on an annual basis (at least) the chief internal auditor will provide a formal opinion to the Board and

top management that addresses the adequacy of governance, risk management and related controls. It will be built on the results of audits included in the plan, and the scope of and basis for the overall opinion will be clearly stated. The CAE will design the audit plan with that in mind. While there is a desire to perform consulting and other engagements that endear internal audit to management (generating tangible cost savings and other results), the primary focus has to be on the work required to provide assurance.

- The audit plan will be a single, integrated plan based on a single, integrated risk assessment. The only risk is business risk, and there is no such thing as IT risk – only the effect of IT-related failures on business risks. Performing a separate IT-risk assessment is wrong. The right approach (in my opinion) is to look at the risks to the objectives of the organization, among which are risks related to failures within IT.

- We also need to build up the courage to take on the topic of governance. The IIA definition of internal auditing requires that we provide assurance on governance, as well as on risk management and the related internal controls. Far too few include governance processes in their audit plans, except as they relate to the code of conduct. This is playing around the edges, instead of taking on the heart of governance, such as the activities of the Board and its committees, including the timeliness and quality of information they receive; the organization and staffing of the enterprise; and the process for establishing, communicating and cascading organizational strategies through the organization – to ensure all managers are working to optimize performance and realize organizational goals.

Fortunately, the IIA's guidance on auditing governance should be available by the time this book is published.

Another good friend who has been outspoken recently is Larry Harrington. The CAE at Raytheon, Larry has been talking up the notion of internal auditors as "rock stars". (He was the kick-off speaker at the GAM – General Audit Management – conference). At least part of this vision is that we become a louder and more influential driver for change within our organizations.

I am pleased to see CAEs driving risk management into their companies. They are frequently the ones who raise the topic with top management, discuss the need with the Board, and explain the need. Often, CAEs are being asked to take on responsibility for risk management – after all, who else within the organization understands it well. We should not be afraid to take this on, whether it is to get it going and then pass it on to a chief risk officer, or to run the program permanently. If we tread carefully, perhaps following the guidance in the IIA UK paper on the role of internal audit in risk management, we can add real value without impairing our objectivity and independence.

One area that CAEs need to focus on and drive change is around the quality, reliability and timeliness of the information used by management and the Board to run the organization. Too many have multiple computer systems that don't play well together, thousands of spreadsheets, and a variety of data warehouses and business intelligence systems. The information used by management and provided to the Board comes from a variety of sources. It needs manipulation and consolidation before it can be used. By the time it is presented to management, it is days if not weeks old. It is also historical, looking at the past and not the future. If there are forecasts, they are not risk adjusted (i.e. adjusted based on the likelihood of various scenarios).

Too often, management is managing by looking into a rear-view mirror. Not only that, but because of the fragmented systems, the rear-view mirror is fractured and so the view of the past is not clear.

Internal audit should recognize this and other inhibitors of optimized performance, and be the rock stars that drive change. When we recognize problems with our systems and data, we should be heard at board and top management levels. We should also be alert and making sure management is paying attention to the possibilities offered by new technology. As Larry says, with urgency, we need to be prepared to take some risks ourselves, loudly advocating the need for change.

Internal auditors should be embracing new technologies themselves, for their own area. Too many are complacent, watching from the sidelines as others – within their own organization – make use of social media for collaboration and risk monitoring, and obtain insight into their operations and performance through business intelligence.

It is time for internal audit functions to commit to change in the tools and methodologies they have embraced for decades. How can CAEs justify standing still when technology has not? Both business intelligence and continuous monitoring/auditing tools have undreamed of capabilities for putting data at auditors' fingertips and monitoring enterprise activities to ensure controls are operating as intended and detect inappropriate activity. Too few internal auditors even know whether their organization owns and uses tools like these (for example, for financial analysis), let alone make full use of them!

Coming back to Richard's question, you may suggest that people don't blame internal auditors because they are not seen as major contributors to organizational governance. Certainly, the profession of internal auditing does not have the prestige of our external-audit colleagues. While leadership at the IIA is rightly concerned with advocacy for the profession and a place of respect for our Institute, I have to ask whether we deserve that respect. Have we earned it?

At too many organizations, internal audit continues to be a subordinate, middle-management operation. I believe there are two interconnected reasons for this:

- Boards have not demanded that we step up and fill their assurance void. While we are useful in detecting and investigating fraud, and reporting on controls in important areas, they don't expect us to provide an overall assessment of governance processes, risk management and the related controls. If they were to drive, the profession would follow.
- Internal audit leaders at most companies have not led the way, educating their boards and showing them that internal audit can fill their assurance void – with formal assessments of governance, risk management and controls. If more CAEs started driving and showing through their example what is possible, then boards will come to expect it and demand a higher level of service from all CAEs.

The way forward requires that we:

- step up and take on the challenge of the Board's assurance gap: provide them with a formal, regular assessment of the condition of governance and risk management processes and the related controls

- demonstrate, through excellence in performance, that we deserve this trust
- be loud rock stars, encouraging and driving change within our organizations
- leverage the promise of technology, so we can extend the quality and breadth of our assurance and consulting services without major increases in budget.

Moving the internal audit profession forward requires leaders. Dan Swanson is one. His massive volume of work, reflected in this book and numerous other writings, helps internal auditors all over the world perform quality audits – and demonstrate the quality and value of our profession.

Norman Marks

Vice President, GRC, SAP BusinessObjects

PART 1: INTERNAL AUDITING

CHAPTER 1: INTRODUCTION TO INTERNAL AUDIT

If someone is going down the wrong road, he doesn't need motivation to speed him up. What he needs is education to turn him around.

Jim Rohn

The internal audit function, from step zero

Internal auditing can provide managers and the Board with valuable assistance by giving objective assurance about their organization's governance, risk management and control processes. Establishing a robust internal audit function is a long-term and worthwhile investment for most organizations because an internal audit department can act as an independent advisor for the Board and senior management. Where an organization has not established an internal audit department, the identification of the benefits and role(s) internal audit could play should be the initial step. Where an internal audit function has been in operation, a review of its recent performance to identify improvement opportunities is recommended.

An executive sponsor is critical

The organization will need an executive sponsor to lead the analysis of the many issues, benefits, costs, activities, and so forth, involved in establishing a new internal audit function. A senior executive from within the organization should drive the research and "business case" efforts with engaged oversight and support being provided by the audit committee.

The first important area to explore is what the role and mandate of the internal audit department should be, that is, what services it should provide and what priorities the function should have. The internal audit charter should support the audit committee's responsibilities, and the long-term internal audit plan should present the assurance plans for the internal audit function and the audit committee.

The assurance requirements of the Board and management will be key drivers for determining internal audit priorities. The chair of the audit committee, the chief executive officer and the chief financial officer will be the three key executives to be interviewed, although other officers certainly should provide ideas and input.

What type of skills will the internal audit function require? Certainly the obvious audit skills will be needed: audit management, project management and strong communication skills. Many others are necessary as well. If technology is integral to the long-term success of the organization, then a strong weighting should be given to IT savvy auditors. If product development is core, then operationally strong auditors should make up a large part of the internal audit staff complement.

A strong knowledge of current and emerging management practices will be absolutely critical for all organizations. Finally, you'll also need to look at the soft skills, including good leadership, effective teamwork and, above all, good people-management skills.

1: Introduction to Internal Audit

Internal audit should be internal to the organization

There are also many options when resourcing the internal audit function, from staffing internally to co-sourcing (blending internal and external resourcing), to starting with an outsourced service while various start-up issues get resolved. Personally, I believe a core internally staffed internal audit function is the best route, with use of selective outsourced or internal subject-matter experts to augment the core group's efforts. Also, during the first few years in particular, the assistance of audit consultants with different backgrounds and expertise can provide valuable contributions to the successful launch of the new audit function. As internal audit is often viewed as an integral part of training for high-potential employees, the organizational design should provide for two-year or other rotational positions.

Audit best practices are important to every internal audit function. Operating below acceptable standards is never acceptable and learning from others' efforts is always strongly recommended. A variety of benchmarking services are available, as well as leading edge information from professional associations and various audit-service providers and vendors that may be helpful. For an existing internal audit function, an external quality-assessment review can provide many helpful suggestions. It is also important that you implement an objective and independent audit function and a solid reporting line to the audit committee – a dotted reporting line to the CEO (chief executive officer) will help meet this need.

Investment in tools, techniques and technology is recommended

The internal audit processes are another important area that must be explored. For example:

- Do you want electronic working-paper files?
- Do you need an audit-management software package?
- What technology requirements will the new function need?

People are your most important resource and, with the internal audit function, this notion is no different. Staffing the function, particularly the chief audit executive (CAE) position, needs to be handled professionally and with an eye towards the long-term requirements of the organization.

The Institute of Internal Auditors has developed a variety of papers and other guidance, including a comprehensive 16-step "roadmap" (for establishing the internal audit function) that includes links to various resources to assist your efforts. The Board, audit committee and executive management must be satisfied that the new internal audit function they implement will be appropriate and add value to the organization. A robust internal audit function strengthens corporate performance and provides assurance to the audit committee and the Board that the organization is doing all the things it should be doing.

Setting long-term goals for internal audit

Internal audit efforts must be risk based and contribute to the long-term assurance needs of the organization and its board. A formal audit risk assessment must be completed at least annually and the results of that assessment should direct audit priorities. In many organizations a focus on short-term results (quarterly financial results and meeting current regulatory requirements) has driven the priorities of management, and consequently the organization, toward a short-term perspective. Similarly, internal auditing's efforts have moved toward this short-term focus, boiling down priorities to whichever audits the company needs to complete in the immediate quarter. The turn of the calendar year is an excellent time to refocus sights on the long-term horizon. For example, what does the organization want to achieve in the next three to five years, and what does it need to do to get there? Certainly, each organization will have different goals, objectives, issues and challenges, and no single "standard" long-term internal audit plan will work; but the below mentioned list is the top 12 internal audit priorities that I would recommend for charting out the long-term internal audit plan.

The top 12 internal-audit priorities

Over the next three to five years, internal audit departments should evaluate their organizations' efforts in the following areas and provide their "opinions" to management and the Board.

- **P1: The enterprise risk management (ERM) program**. To my thinking, ERM is a silver bullet for improving governance and organizational results because it identifies your key objectives – and managing risks that accompany those objectives is effective governance. Whether your organization is a proponent of ISO31000; the Committee of Sponsoring Organizations of the Treadway Commission's (COSO's) risk management framework; the governance, risk and compliance GRC capability model from the Open Compliance and Ethics Group (OCEG); or other standards, it is time for organizations to take ERM to the next level. Completing an internal audit of the organization's ERM efforts will provide everyone with a baseline assessment report that also will reveal gaps in risk management.

- **P2: The top three most significant business initiatives.** Over the past 15 years I have promoted (indeed, strongly encouraged) the auditing of the top three most significant IT initiatives. This year and going forward, I now firmly believe in auditing the three most significant business initiatives, with a very robust analysis of the IT component for each of these initiatives.

- **P3: The business continuity program (BCP) and the disaster recovery program (DRP).** BCP and DRP are on everyone's list of top 10 priorities; the problem is that they always rank in the bottom half. It is now time to ensure that the organization's resiliency efforts are truly operational. Establishing a robust preparedness capability is also one of the best investments an organization can make; auditing BCP and DRP efforts will assist the organization greatly in ensuring that the proper attention is given. An effective business continuity capability is absolutely essential, although being able to recover IT is, of course, critical.

- **P4: The information-security program efforts.** Protection of an organization's assets is a critical activity; for some companies it is the most critical activity. Auditing an information-security program is also a long-term effort involving many audits over many years, and it is time to start that long-term assurance effort. A very simple starting test: has the effectiveness of your security efforts been discussed at the Board level this year?

- **P5: The overall governance regime.** Corporate governance; organizational governance; performance accountability; governance, risk and compliance (GRC) – governance goes by many names. Internal auditing provides assurances to management and the Board regarding an organization's governance, risk management and controls processes. Therefore, fundamentally, internal audit should provide an opinion regarding the overall governance "regime," regardless of the exact term your company uses to describe its efforts. Also verify that sustainable development and corporate social-responsibility issues are included in the governance structure.

- **P6: The compliance and ethics program efforts.** Compliance and ethics efforts have received enormous attention (and funding) during the last five years, and this will continue over the next five years. Depending on the internal audit department's past efforts, audits of the compliance and ethics programs should either drill down into specific opportunities or zoom out to a high level to provide an overall assessment.

- **P7: Records management.** Some people may disagree with including this item on my list, or ranking it so highly. My point for including it is that if your organization has not started upgrading its records-management program to reflect today's regulatory requirements and technological capabilities, then the organization is "at risk." An audit of the records-management program will assist in the determination of what opportunities for improvement exist, as well as risks. There is nothing worse than the legal nightmare of having a policy and not following it.

- **P8: The quality of the enterprise information for decision making**. Information is critical to every organizational effort. The quality of the organization's information will directly affect organizational results and, therefore, should be assessed on a regular basis – by management and by internal audit. The assessment should include the quality and completeness of the information, as well as the assumptions and analysis. Information management will become more critical every year.

- **P9: The anti-fraud program**. Sarbanes-Oxley (and equivalent governance-related legislation elsewhere) was passed to reduce the occurrence and impact of fraud and to increase the reliability and integrity of financial statements and related management assertions. Anti-fraud programs need to be established (or strengthened) as a result of these new governance requirements. The Board and management need to know that these programs work effectively.

- **P10: The IT function's efforts to meet business needs**. This audit priority is extremely diverse. The IT function performs a broad range of services and it has a substantial impact on business results. As a consequence, the IT audit priorities require a more detailed risk assessment to determine what the audit priorities should be. Fundamentally, evaluating the IT function's efforts to meet business needs is a core audit requirement. Assessing IT's effectiveness, efficiency and "customer service" are the three main components of an effective IT shop. Deciding on further IT audit "focus" beyond these areas needs to be based on a more formal audit IT-risk assessment.

- **P11: Board and executive management service requests (consulting and assurance projects)**. This audit activity is an important catch-all to assist with the specific or unique needs of the organization. It is also included in my top dozen to highlight the need for a customer service "philosophy" by the internal audit function. The percentage of the audit budget allocated to this important activity will differ widely, but it lets the Board and management know that internal audit is responsive to the Board's assurance and consulting needs. Of course, these "special" audit projects should be of significant value to the organization, and they should not distract from the delivery of the overall audit commitment.

- **P12: Process management, including continuous process improvement**. My last audit priority relates to improving organizational performance. I label this audit priority "process management"; your company might call it a Six Sigma program, while others might call it a corporate quality-management initiative. This audit priority is focused on encouraging and confirming that there is an organizational process-improvement program in place, whatever the title. If the organization has not established an organizational program to improve its performance on a sustainable basis, it is at risk.

Defining the long term

As mentioned previously, each organization is different, and its internal audit priorities will be different, too. Still, for any organization, internal audit's priorities should be risk based and should focus on the organization's governance, risk management and control processes. Corporate-wide "themes" of cost efficiency, cost effectiveness, strategic management and control, quality management, process improvement, and so forth, will (and should) influence your internal audit efforts over coming years. You also should ensure that the internal audit plan has a strong linkage with the organization's strategic plan.

> **The bottom line:** it is time for executives to lead, managers to manage, boards to govern, and auditors to provide assurances to the Board and management that things are as people say they are. Your next audit planning effort should make this clear – to everyone.

What is internal auditing?

In my line of work, I'm often asked exactly what internal auditing is supposed to be. According to the *International Standards for the Professional Practice of Internal Auditing*, the answer is pretty straightforward: "Internal auditing is an independent, objective assurance and consulting activity designed to add value and improve an organization's operations."

You might want an answer more expansive than those 19 words. So, let's take a step back from the fine points of executing internal audits, to reacquaint ourselves with what internal audit is and how you can make it helpful to your job. Internal auditing provides opportunities for companies to improve based on independent analysis and advice. Internal audit also helps the Board and senior management to monitor the organization. To preserve the integrity and independence of audits, auditors maintain a delicate balance between offering advice (mainly consulting services) and providing opinions about a process, system, account balance, or other subject matter (assurance services).

The size and complexity of internal auditing functions are as diverse as the range of operating environments, risk appetites, and business and audit objectives that a company can have. The scope of audits can also vary from project to project within a company, depending on an auditor's focus (for example, on high-risk business processes, or key management and technical controls). Ensuring appropriate audit focus is one of many reasons that management should communicate with auditors, and *vice versa*, early and often for every audit project.

What does internal audit do?

Internal auditing provides unbiased information to management and the Board to help them make better decisions. Internal-audit conclusions and recommendations are based primarily on independently gathered evidence and knowledge. For example, when evaluating information security, the internal auditor informs the Board and management about whether:

- business units understand the importance of security and are adhering to policies
- key information assets and systems are sufficiently secure
- programs exist to update and strengthen safeguards constantly against internal and external security threats
- the organization's policies are reasonable.

The internal auditor might also independently validate that the organization's information security efforts are proactive and effective against current and emerging threats. To provide this level of assurance, the internal auditor may compare current organizational practices with industry practices and regulatory guidelines. Notably, auditing provides only a reasonable level of assurance. Auditors cannot provide an insurance policy against every possible fault or deficiency, particularly regarding activities that cannot be totally controlled, such as collusion or management override.

What is management's role?

An internal audit engagement typically has three phases: planning, fieldwork and reporting. While internal audit drives the process, management has a vital role to play in each one. During *planning*, senior management should first focus on the audit plan (the auditor's "roadmap") and ensure that business managers understand audit's purpose, focus and approach. An open, positive discussion with the audit team regarding these defining factors helps both management and the audit team communicate their expectations up front.

Audit planning should focus on critical or sensitive risks, but all risks should be considered. To this end, active involvement by management in audit planning can contribute to the overall success of an audit. Management should ensure that things they consider to be risks are addressed by the audit plan. Both the auditor and management should be identifying areas of risk. Management should also discuss the evaluation criteria auditors will use to assess the activity being audited. Lastly, managers and auditors should broadly discuss planned audit testing, although auditors must have the authority and discretion to select tests they deem appropriate and the transactions being audited.

During *fieldwork*, management facilitates the auditors' access to appropriate people, systems and facilities. Management should confirm the presentation of the facts by the internal auditor, ensuring that the auditors have considered all the information available. The audit-team leader and senior executives of the areas being audited should meet regularly – perhaps even weekly, and at a minimum at least once during each audit phase – to discuss audit progress, identified issues and potential actions. An open dialogue between senior members of both management and the audit team does much to avert misunderstandings and resolve disputed findings before the audit team issues its draft report. The audit team should communicate critical findings to management as early as possible, even outside of the established meeting schedule. These findings may also be reviewed during regular meetings, but prompt notice is necessary and usually appreciated.

During *reporting*, the internal audit team communicates its analysis and recommendations. Management receives and reviews the findings, develops corrective actions and may even begin implementing changes. Management should ensure the presentation of the findings is appropriate. They should also determine whether or not they are willing to accept the level of risk identified. If not, they should develop a realistic action plan with specific goals and timelines. Managers shouldn't agree to recommendations that they can't actually do. (Too often I see management agreeing and, in the same breath, saying: "We will put in a business case to get the necessary resources." If they don't have the resources, they're not in agreement.) If, on the other hand, the company is willing to accept the risk, this should be clearly stated.

The bottom line

Audits exist to assess how well a business unit meets the performance goals of the organization, as dictated by the CEO, CFO (chief financial officer), board, investors and others. Accordingly, management's goal is to demonstrate how well operations, controls and results meet the needs of the business. During audit planning, managers should work with the auditors to ensure the audit scope, goals and objectives are appropriate. Thus, a prompt response to the auditors' requests for information and records throughout the audit process – planning, testing and reporting – is for the benefit of the business, not its auditors.

Auditors exist to provide the Board and senior management with an objective, independent assessment of a business unit or program (such as information security), including what they see as key opportunities for improvement. To prepare their opinions and conclusions, auditors need to review evidence of the risk management efforts and assess performance. If managers are able to demonstrate performance and show that accountability has been established and effectively discharged, it will result in a positive audit report. It's that simple.

The ultimate goal of management throughout the audit process should be to demonstrate that their efforts meet the expectations of the CEO, Board of Directors and investors. Likewise, the auditor's requests should be aligned with these overarching needs; that is, to support responsible performance within a sound and ethical business environment. Accordingly, auditors and managers should work to help each other reach common goals – auditors striving to earnestly, honestly and competently assess program effectiveness, and management working to help auditors to complete valid assessments. In that vein, auditors always look for sound management practices.

Always remember that managers, not auditors, are responsible for defining and implementing solutions to issues found in the audit. Thus, it is in everyone's best interest to have a cooperative, collaborative audit process that respects the independence and discretion of all participants. Auditors should listen to management, and for its part, management should encourage staff to be open and honest with auditors.

Have you talked with your auditor lately?

CHAPTER 2: THE PROFESSIONAL PRACTICE OF INTERNAL AUDIT

Quality is never an accident; it is always the result of high intention, sincere effort, intelligent direction, and skillful execution; it presents the wise choice of many alternatives.

William A Foster

20 questions for directors to ask internal auditors

The internal audit department's unique position within a company provides management and audit committee members with valuable assistance, by giving objective assurance on governance, risk management and control processes. Audit committees, of course, are responsible for providing oversight to the internal audit efforts within the organization – so how audit committees work with their internal audit staff is crucial to the success of the entire internal audit operation.

As one of the cornerstones of corporate governance (along with the Board of Directors, senior management and external auditing), internal auditing can provide strategic, operational and tactical value to an organization's operations. For example, internal auditing is:

- A resource to the Board and management for helping to ensure the entire organization has the resources, systems, and processes for operating an efficient and effective organization.
- An assurance service for management and the Board that confirms adequate controls are in place. By ensuring that qualified professional reviews and tests are performed,

the Board and management can advance their goals of overseeing the organization's operations and helping to ensure continuous improvement and success.

• An independent validation that the organization's efforts are proactive and effective against current and emerging threats.

Without question, fostering a strong internal audit department should be a high priority for the audit committee. Audit-committee members should have input to the leadership and activities of their internal audit team, as well as oversee the internal audit team's performance. The Institute of Internal Auditors' briefing paper, *Internal Audit Standards: Why They Matter*, provides a summary of typical audit-committee responsibilities for oversight of internal audit functions, and discusses how audit committees can forge closer ties with their internal auditors. At companies where an internal audit function has not been formally established, these questions can be discussed with senior management to deliver that same sense of urgency.

Questions to ask

How to get started? The IIA has another briefing paper, *20 Questions Directors Should Ask of Internal Audit*, to help audit committees develop a better understanding of their expectations and the chief auditing executive's duties. (The questions themselves, organized into six categories, are listed at the end of this section.)

The first important area to explore is what the role and mandate of the internal audit department should be – that is, what services it should provide and what priorities the function should have. The internal audit charter should support the audit-committee's responsibilities, and the long-term internal audit plan should present the assurance plans for the organization and the audit committee.

The second important area to explore is the relationship of the audit committee with the internal audit function. Here the key issues are whether the internal audit activities are supported by the audit committee (for example, ensuring appropriate organizational status and sufficient resources), and what influence management has on the internal audit function through its organizational structure. If the internal audit department reports administratively to a level deep down in the organization, experience has shown its work could be adversely affected by senior management.

A third topic is resources. Does internal auditing have the appropriate level of resources, and the right skill sets to do its job well? If not, auditing of the organization and the depth of analysis can be inappropriate. Investment in internal audit activities is worthwhile, but a regular dialogue on what level of support works best between the audit committee and the chief internal auditor ensures a healthy internal audit function.

Discussions around internal audit processes are useful to ensure the internal audit function is adopting best practices, improving itself and – most importantly – tackling the right projects in the right ways. Just as external auditors evaluate business areas during financial audits, audit-committee members must be confident that internal auditing is always improving too.

Finally, the results of the internal audit efforts should be regularly reviewed, and an overall determination made about whether the audit committee is satisfied with the information and performance it receives from internal auditing.

Directors must satisfy themselves that the answers they receive are appropriate, and that the internal audit function works. Increased communication between the audit committee and the leadership of the internal audit function is the first step, certainly, but meaningful dialogue is necessary to support the internal audit function and take it to the next level of success.

A robust internal audit function strengthens corporate performance and provides assurance to the audit committee and the Board that the organization is doing all the things it should be doing. The audit committee also needs to provide effective oversight of this important function – and the resources and questions highlighted today will support efforts to do just that. As Eleanor Bloxham, chief executive of the Corporate Governance Alliance and adviser to companies and boards, puts it: "A close relationship between audit committees and internal audit isn't optional; it's the lynchpin of an organization's safety and soundness."

The excerpt below is taken from *20 Questions Directors Should Ask about Internal Audit*, published by the Canadian Institute of Chartered Accountants (CICA):

A. Internal audit's role and mandate

1 Should we have an Internal Audit function?
2 What should our Internal Audit function do?
3 What should be the mandate of the Internal Audit function?

B. Internal audit relationships

4 What is the relationship between Internal Auditing and the Audit Committee?
5 To whom does Internal Auditing report administratively?

C. Internal audit resources

6 How is the Internal Audit function staffed?
7 How does Internal Auditing get and maintain the expertise it
   needs to conduct its assignments?
8 Are the activities of Internal Auditing appropriately
   coordinated with those of the external auditors?

D. Internal audit process

9 How is the Internal Audit plan developed?
10 What does the Internal Audit plan not cover?
11 How are Internal Audit findings reported?
12 How are corporate managers required to respond to Internal
   Audit findings and recommendations?
13 What services does Internal Auditing provide in connection
   with fraud?
14 How do you assess the effectiveness of your Internal Audit
   function?

E. Closing questions

15 Does Internal Auditing have sufficient resources?
16 Does the Internal Audit function get appropriate support from
   the CEO and senior management team?
17 Are you satisfied that this organization has adequate internal
   controls over its major risks?
18 Are there any other matters that you wish to bring to the Audit
   Committee's attention?
19 Are there other ways in which Internal Auditing and the Audit
   Committee could support each other?

F. Audit committee overall assessment

20 Are we (the Audit Committee) satisfied with our Internal Audit
   function?

Giving the finance department the audit it deserves

Usually I write about how to audit some aspect of a whole
enterprise – say, how the company manages risk, or how
executives invest their IT dollars. That's important, but we

shouldn't lose sight of the nuts and bolts. Companies are run by specific departments doing specific jobs, and they need auditing too. Therefore, we're going to get back to our internal auditing roots and focus on the finance department. The finance function is critical because it helps drive most organizations to higher levels of performance.

A well-run finance department enables sound financial management, strategic planning, organizational performance reporting, treasury-related activities and financial reporting (among many other things). It tells you how many dollars are coming and going and where they're coming *from* and going *to*. Without that information, people are driving blindfolded, and the organization will have a difficult time sustaining long-term value. The bottom line is that by focusing your audits *only* on financial reporting, significant activities within the finance function could be inappropriately or inadvertently ignored by executive management and the Board. Key opportunities for growth and improvement could also be missed.

Characteristics of a world-class finance organization

Where do you start? Obtain agreement on what the characteristics of a world-class finance function within your company should look like. Based on research published by the Government Accountability Office (GAO), "the finance department" can best be defined in terms of the business outcomes it produces – outcomes such as: improved business analysis, innovative solutions to business problems, reduced operating costs, increased capabilities to perform *ad-hoc* analysis, and improved overall business performance. To build a world-class finance function and help achieve better business outcomes, organizations need to define the finance function's agenda – that is, get a consensus on finance's mission, vision, core values, and goals and strategies – and craft a plan to get there.

The GAO has taken that high-level foundational effort even further, by outlining four broad goals and a total of 11 best practices that define a value-creating, customer-focused finance function that delivers real business results. They are:

Goal (1): Make financial management an entity-wide priority

- **Practice 1**: Build a foundation of control and accountability.
- **Practice 2**: Provide clear, strong executive leadership.
- **Practice 3**: Use training to change the culture and engage line managers.

Goal (2): Redefine the role of finance

- **Practice 4**: Assess the finance organization's current role in meeting enterprise objectives.
- **Practice 5**: Maximize the efficiency of day-to-day accounting activities.
- **Practice 6**: Organize finance to add value.

Goal (3): Provide meaningful information to decision makers

- **Practice 7**: Develop systems that support the partnership between finance and operations.
- **Practice 8**: Re-engineer processes in conjunction with new technology.
- **Practice 9**: Translate financial data into meaningful performance information (e.g. develop exhibits and

dashboards that clearly communicate financial performance and its impacts on the organization).

Goal (4): Build a team that delivers results

- **Practice 10**: Develop a finance team with the right mix of skills and competencies.
- **Practice 11**: Build a finance organization that attracts and retains talent.

While many finance functions have focused almost entirely on financial reporting – and make no mistake, that's a large and critical part of their job – a high-performance company needs to position the organization for the future, by building all the finance capabilities that are needed going forward.

Audit finance to improve organizational performance

Internal audit's evaluation of the finance function can provide valuable feedback to the Board and executive management. An audit of the finance department should determine whether or not the function's current services are appropriate, whether performance is continuously being optimized, whether management and finance are working together, and whether finance is helping the company recognize and respond to new business opportunities as they arise. There are many issues worth exploring in an audit of finance; a few of the important ones are presented below. The audit team will need to complete a comprehensive audit plan to determine the correct focus and priorities for an internal audit of the finance function. Remember, the goal of an internal audit should be meeting the assurance needs of the Board and executive management.

- Does the finance function help management define, and agree upon, strategy? Does it help with implementation of that strategy, including management's recognition of, and response to, new and emerging business opportunities? Auditors should investigate how accounting and operational performance data is being used to support budget formulation and strategic planning.
- Do budgeting processes support the assignment of management accountability and monitoring of performance? The audit team should investigate whether the finance function helps top management with forward-looking analyses of the numbers and by forging strong ties between accounting information, budget formulation and capital investment, and strategic planning and implementation. A high-performance company needs to position the organization for the future, by building all of the finance capabilities that are needed going forward.
- Are there appropriate systems, policies, procedures and guidelines relating to financial management? How successful is the finance department in meeting business needs? The audit could explore how much line managers value good financial management and information in the execution of their various duties. Managers must constantly leverage and make the "best use" of the monies, staff and other resources they have under their responsibility; deferring financial decisions to strictly the folks in finance is not a good practice.
- Has the finance team done everything necessary to get a grip on the organization's financial needs? While everyone is trying to forecast the next disaster to "handle," in my view, process improvement and

constantly strengthening the company's key capabilities is a vital long-term approach to improving resiliency and overall performance.

- Are all of the finance functions performing well? The audit team should ensure the organization's functions have been defined: accounts payable, payroll, performance reporting, performance analysis, budgeting, and so forth. Confirm that assessment criteria are available to evaluate those groups' performance during the audit. A client satisfaction survey or formal external benchmarking could also be useful in completing an audit assessment of overall functional performance. Consider performing a strategic Strengths-Weaknesses-Opportunities-Threats (SWOT) analysis based on a portfolio of historical and plausible future events. The outcome of a SWOT analysis will identify specific and actionable key opportunities for improvements and growth.

- Do the financial practices of the organization meet generally accepted and industry-accepted financial management standards? Compliance with accounting and auditing standards is important, and an internal audit of finance should usually include a review of the organization's accounting policies and practices. Where departures in accounting policy or practice do arise – and sometimes an exception to common practice does make sense for a specific company – has that departure been explained and approved by the proper managers?

Organizations must proactively improve capabilities

An internal audit of finance should foremost identify key improvement opportunities. The audit should confirm that long-term finance needs (financial management, treasury management, or anything else) are identified and being addressed. Equally important, the audit should make sure that the finance department can track all the dollars floating around the company. Is cash management and bookkeeping strong? What can be improved?

Lastly, the audit should investigate who is driving organizational capability improvement efforts and assess whether those efforts are working well. Finance is not only about internal control over financial reporting, nor is it only about quarterly and annual reporting; while these activities are important, they do not significantly affect long-term value creation. A good finance function is about much more than that. A good audit of the finance function is about much more than that, too.

How to weigh IT investment decisions

Corporate management has always been told to invest wisely in IT. The Board has always been told to ensure management invests wisely in IT. It is a truism everyone states all the time. Too frequently, however, IT investment decisions by management and the Board have relied on, and even deferred to, managers of the IT function. That results in what I call the Black Hole approach to IT investment: throw enough money into technology, and we'll get something of value in the end. Corporations can, and must, do better than that. IT is now central to every core business process, and core business processes are central to sound governance. Can more formal, cohesive decisions about IT investment, therefore, improve your corporate governance? I think so – but those decisions must be directed by the *business* managers, not the *technology* managers. The

Board and executive management must also constantly monitor the company's significant IT expenditures and participate in all major IT investment decisions.

For years, business has encouraged IT to focus on delivering business priorities. At the same time, IT has tried to be an integral part of business planning and align IT efforts and investments with business priorities. At the end of the day, effective IT investment really does require the ongoing and engaged involvement of all key participants. Decisions regarding IT investment in your compliance and other governance initiatives should be driven by management and the Board; IT managers should only be providing advice and counsel.

Where does one start? The company's strategic planning effort should be the first place to look; that is, the Board and senior management need to define their strategic direction, key priorities, objectives, and draw up a "roadmap" to get there. After all, if the company hasn't defined where it wants to go, all the IT investment in the world won't help it get there.

Apply that same discipline when contemplating governance and compliance. What goals does the business want to achieve? How can IT help it meet them? Answer those questions, and then start mapping out your various compliance and governance efforts and the core IT needs; that is your blueprint to guide your IT investment decisions.

The IT department's role

IT planning efforts must be integrated with a company's business plans. Since business plans change and priorities evolve, the IT function needs an *investment management process*, so it can continually refine its own priorities as the overall business priorities evolve. IT also needs to acquaint the business with what is currently possible, and at what price. IT needs to explain the consequences and opportunities the business direction imposes on technology.

If not actively involved in the strategic planning processes, IT management, at a minimum, needs to understand the company's strategic directions and plans in detail. Simply reading strategy papers will not suffice, since important elements of business strategy often aren't written down. Think about who really develops strategy at the company, and cultivate a conversation with those people. Engaging with the company's strategic-development and investment-management processes is one of the most important roles of the CIO and other senior IT executives. Particularly for compliance and governance efforts, IT needs to be aware of best practices in the industry – a topic most IT managers don't know all that well, frankly – and bring forward innovative solutions to tackle problems, such as increased regulatory reporting requirements, endless refinements to the compliance and ethics program's information needs, and so on.

Finally, by matching IT investment decisions to the company's long-term business plans, IT can go beyond the chronic problem of having too few resources for the current budget cycle. With a longer perspective in mind, the inevitable tactical quick-fix imperatives can be balanced against genuine strategic IT initiatives. Prioritizing and coordinating IT investments needs this broader view. IT also needs to deliver its own assessments of opportunities and threats and work with the company on how to mitigate (or take advantage) of them.

Key takeaways:

- The CIO and other senior IT executives should actively participate in the organization's business planning.
- The organization's leadership should be involved in IT strategic planning and investment management activities.
- The Board should ask management to describe how business planning and IT planning are being integrated, and encourage frequent and ongoing dialogue between board members, the management team and IT leadership.

The internal auditor's role

Although achieving and maintaining IT business alignment is really a management issue, the internal audit department can help. Internal audit evaluation of an organization's strategic planning efforts, including how IT supports the business priorities, can provide valuable feedback to the Board and senior management. An audit of IT investment processes should determine whether:

- significant business priorities are appropriately identified and assessed on an ongoing basis
- changes to those priorities are monitored
- significant investment management controls are operating effectively and consistently
- risk management techniques are in place and effective
- management and staff have the processes in place to recognize and respond to new business opportunities as they arise
- IT-related investments are effectively and efficiently managed.

There are two distinct elements to most audits of IT-investment management. First, the auditor evaluates the specification, design and implementation of the IT-investment management processes. Then the auditor examines how the IT investment management processes actually operate, including an assessment of the business priorities currently being addressed.

How would this improve IT investments in compliance and governance? By helping to ensure the organization is defining its business priorities and has an investment process that aligns IT expenditures to those priorities.

Four critical issues to evaluate

Issue 1: Does management have a strategic IT plan in place that is updated regularly and supports the annual plans, budgets and prioritization of the various IT efforts?

Ideally, an IT strategic plan would be developed and approved by the Board, although the IT planning document may take many forms. It could be a separate IT plan, something combined with the organization's overall business plan, or a series of business case submissions over time.

An overall strategic planning process regarding IT investment and IT spending prioritization should exist. Always remember that business planning should drive the IT priorities and IT investment decisions: that's critical. Successful projects happen when business management retains control of the initiative and sets clear and balanced business requirements.

Issue 2: What level of investment in IT (and IT security) has occurred in the past two to three years? What is planned for the coming two to three years? Is there a reasonable level of expenditure, compared to the overall operating and capital budgets?

While no specific level of investment in IT can be labeled "appropriate," management should be able to explain the reasonableness of the IT and IT security expenditures in relation to the overall capital and operating budgets. The IT expenditure trend should be in line with the business and IT plans. A key board concern is always whether the company is spending too much or too little on IT and IT security.

Issue 3: Have the roles and responsibilities for IT management and oversight of IT investment, been defined and assigned within the company?

The responsibilities for the various IT activities within the organization related to IT management and IT investment should be defined and assigned to specific personnel. There should be a logical allocation of IT responsibilities within the organization.

Issue 4: Does management monitor IT's performance, as well as IT's capability to continue providing the services the company relies on?

What are the major issues reported to senior management regarding IT and IT security? Is there a healthy debate at the Board level regarding concerns raised by management or the Board? If not, what could be done to improve the situation? This question also explores the operational monitoring that is performed by management regarding IT operations – and whether IT is outsourced or managed internally, it should be occurring.

Practices that support alignment

Key management practices driving more effective alignment, and consequently improving IT investment results, have been identified by the IT Process Institute. They include:

- identify opportunities to use emerging technology to meet business objectives
- have an effective process and methodology for justifying and prioritizing IT investment decisions
- develop and enforce enterprise infrastructure standards
- have a project management office function to provide oversight to business prioritized IT projects
- have a formal periodic process for the IT department to identify what is needed by the business.

Oversight of IT investment must be integrated into a company's ongoing strategic planning effort, to ensure IT efforts consistently contribute to the organization's priorities. Executive management should revisit how it defines IT investment priorities, and the Board should encourage a review of current practices to identify key improvement priorities. With limited funds available, investments in IT for compliance and governance improvement must be balanced with other competing priorities; involving all key stakeholders in that reconciliation will help move the organization forward. There should also be an organizational culture that encourages IT and the business to work together continually.

The tipping point for board oversight of IT

Traditionally, and properly, a company's board of directors has focused on governing the organization; that is, the Board ensures that the right CEO is in place, that the right business strategies have been developed, that performance is reported regularly and trending properly, and that the right questions are being asked of management. The Board's agenda is truly endless, and it is absolutely critical that the Board does not micromanage the CEO, attempt to "manage" the organization, or have items on its agenda that are not focused on the long-term success of the organization. The Board should revisit its mandate periodically, reconfirming its roles and responsibilities.

We need to pose the question of what the Board's oversight role is regarding information technology. There is no one right answer to this question, it can even be said the short answer is, "It depends." Indeed, many believe it is not the purview of the Board to discuss IT strategy; the Board is there to provide oversight to management's efforts, and since IT is only a "tool" in achieving those business strategies, in general, it should not be on the Board's agenda. At the other end of the spectrum there are those who maintain that IT is the business for most organizations today, and that as IT goes, so goes the company.

Therefore, the Board needs to be informed and participate in discussions about IT investments, including the organization's IT strategies, plans and processes. Finally, there are others who believe IT or IT security will be the source of our next Enron-style corporate malfeasance, so the Board needs to be much more active with IT and IT security efforts.

Revisit, review, reconsider

My recommendation is that the Board should review and define its oversight role regarding IT. That is, the Board should understand how important the IT activities are to the organization's implementation of business strategies, what IT initiatives are critical to the organization's success, what the strengths and weaknesses of the IT management team are, and what, if any, changes should be instituted regarding the Board oversight of IT.

A basic focus of the Board is ensuring corporate viability, and protecting and increasing shareholder value. If IT is so critical today to the long-term success of the company, then the Board should provide oversight of IT. The Board should *not* get involved in day-to-day management, but it *must* maintain active oversight. IT is a key contributor to the organization's results, including the always visible financial reporting and disclosure effort – and we all know what happens with incorrect financial reporting.

A fundamental question for each organization to investigate and answer is whether board oversight of IT is a "missing piece to the puzzle" in its board governance, or if it is a non-issue for that organization. While the answer is most likely somewhere in the middle of these two extremes, it is up to the Board to decide its mandate, including its roles, responsibilities and various oversight processes. The industry involved can be a factor regarding the degree of oversight needed. Obviously, an IT company and others in the technology sector should consider having a few board directors with IT expertise. Such companies probably need greater board oversight over IT strategy and investments than others, with some even having a board-level technology committee. There are actually few industries today where IT governance is not significant, although the financial, health and technology sectors certainly require more oversight than others.

Defining the Board's IT oversight role

Why is board oversight of IT so important today? Consider:

- The growing extent that corporate productivity is now related to "intellectual capital." With IT so essential to creating organizational value, boards need to understand IT better. That isn't captured through monitoring other, more traditional, areas.
- Productivity growth statistics and estimates of how much of that growth is caused by smart use of IT. Everyone is in a competitive business, and IT can give companies a competitive advantage.

Just because the Board has not taken an active role in IT in the past or put IT on the Board agenda very frequently, that does not mean there isn't a place for the Board regarding IT. It's always better to decide the Board's role going forward than to have it dictated by the next Enron that occurs. I also believe that periodically revisiting the Board's mandate and its various committees' terms of reference is a productive activity in this never-ending effort to improve governance and organizational performance. At the end of the day, isn't that what it is all about?

The Board's governance of the company as it relates to IT will depend on the nature of the organization and also of risks, both strategic and tactical. The Board's involvement is likely to vary over time. The Board's involvement in IT should be driven in the same way as it gets involved in marketing, personnel, legal and other departments – in that there is no "automatic" involvement in IT. You must decide your board's involvement and then act to achieve it.

Governance is fundamentally about identifying and managing strategic risk to the organization, whether that's the risk of the CEO turning out to be a crook, or the business strategy itself being flawed. If the organization doesn't use IT, there's obviously no risk. If the organization has enterprise-level investment in (and dependence on) information and IT, then there is risk. It is the *scale* of the risk that determines whether or not board oversight is necessary. Small risk: who cares? Big risk, think betting the firm on a technology project, then the Board had better oversee it. The Board doesn't need to oversee day-to-day management of IT (other than perhaps agreeing the criteria for recruiting the CIO), but we might think that there are half a dozen key performance indicators that we want to see on a regular basis that tells us how well this part of the business is being managed. There is no hard and fast rule beyond managing risk; which board wants to be on duty when an IT project leads to the company going down? Crying, "We left it to management!" will be just another way of saying, "Please sue us, because we took our fees, but we just weren't paying attention."

In my view, board oversight of IT is essential. For an ever-wider range of industries, IT is too important to be left to technologists alone. That said, the Board must limit the nature of its involvement to strategic issues. The Board should not be involved in where to draw the line in each case, but it should be sure that management is aware of the need to weigh the pros and cons and make an explicit decision in each case. The decision is basically one to be made on business grounds with a proper understanding of the potential, the risks and the constraints of available technology. Too often the business dimension will not even be considered, if these decisions are left to technology experts alone. Has your organization reached its tipping point?

Auditing ethics and compliance programs

Broadly understood, compliance is an important mechanism that helps make governance effective. Monitoring and maintaining compliance is not just to keep the regulators happy; compliance with regulatory requirements and the organization's own policies is a critical component of effective risk management. It is one of the most important ways an organization achieves its business goals, maintains its ethical health, supports its long-term prosperity, and preserves and promotes its values. An effective compliance and ethics program is best organized as integrated processes, assigned to designated business functions and managed by individuals who have overall responsibility and accountability. Compliance can be a daunting challenge, but it is also an opportunity to establish and promote operational effectiveness throughout the entire organization.

The Board and management periodically need to evaluate the design and operating effectiveness of the company's compliance and ethics program. Such evaluations supplement the ongoing, day-to-day monitoring of responses and control activities. Not only do these reviews – audits, really – provide for a more in-depth analysis of the program's design and effectiveness; they also provide an opportunity to consider new practices and technologies that may have been developed since the program was first implemented.

Determining key risks

Defining objectives of the internal audit is the first and one of the most critical steps in setting the audit direction, because it defines the level of assurance with which the Board and management will be provided. From the start, then, internal audit staff should hold discussions with management and the Board (or the audit committee and legal counsel, as necessary) regarding the assurance needs of the key stakeholders to ensure the audit meets the assurance needs of the organization – and it should all be done prior to finishing the audit plan. Compliance and ethics programs cover a very broad span of activities, and the planning phase needs to ensure the proper focus of the audit efforts. The audit should be based on a comprehensive audit risk assessment – that is, auditors must determine what the key risks of the company's compliance and ethics program are. The participation of legal counsel in the audit is another critical factor that should be decided here, during the audit planning (or subsequently, if the plan's assumptions turn out to differ from the actual audit situation). If wrongdoing is identified during the internal audit a dialogue with legal counsel is needed – indeed, it is often critical.

What objectives to set? Three goals should be:

- **Goal 1: Application.** To determine whether the compliance and ethics program provides reasonable assurance of compliance with organizational policies and applicable laws and regulations.
- **Goal 2: Documentation.** To determine whether the program's management framework is documented, in place, and appropriately resourced to meet the organization's needs.

- **Goal 3: Implementation**. To determine whether the program has been implemented effectively, and that its performance reporting system has been defined and accurately presents the results of the program's efforts.

Some key issues to explore during the audit include ensuring that there is:

- **Universality**: Consistency and integration of compliance and ethics programs among different business units within the organization.
- **Integration**: Coordination between the central compliance and ethics office and individual business units.
- **Accountability**: A clear and effective division of roles and responsibilities among the ethics office, compliance, HR, legal and other relevant units.

Down to business

Any internal audit has three phases: planning, fieldwork and reporting. Audits of compliance and ethics programs are no different. During the planning phase, the internal audit team should ensure that all key issues are considered, that the audit objectives will meet the organization's assurance needs, and that the compliance and ethics program is well understood. It is extremely important that the audit focus on evaluating the significant components of a compliance and ethics program; that is, auditors should use a risk-based approach to find the program's elements most likely to fail and in most need of attention. The planning phase is an opportunity to confirm that the audit scope is appropriate, and the cost won't give anyone heartburn.

In the fieldwork phase, the team analyzes the compliance program's various components, based on the goals and methodologies identified in the planning phase. Some of the most important questions relate to: how the Board sets its "tone at the top"; how it communicates those values to employees; how employees at all levels of the company perceive management's commitment to those values; and how the company handles compliance or ethics issues that arise from compliance failures. Audit tests could include: reviewing employee files for signed Code of Conduct or training confirmations; looking at training materials and training program results; reviewing responses to violations; conducting surveys and reviewing the results of them; reviewing management's communications to employees for ethical content; quantifying the organizational resources available for program operation; and assessing the quality of the support for the program's performance reporting.

The reporting phase involves the internal audit team ensuring that all stakeholders are properly informed of the audit results and any management plans to improve the compliance and ethics program. A well-planned and executed internal audit (phase 1 and 2) should make audit reporting straightforward: tell them what you did, what you found, and what management plans to do about it. That's all there is to it.

Internal auditors must take a risk-based approach while planning a compliance and ethics program audit. With limited resources, auditors simply have no choice, but to focus on the highest-risk areas and always strive to add value to the organization. Audit best practices suggest internal auditors should be involved throughout the program's life cycle, not just in post-implementation program evaluations. The internal audit of a compliance and ethics program also needs to be part of a larger overall audit plan. Internal auditors should craft a plan that meets the long-term assurance requirements of the Board and management. A series of internal audits to manage complexity (if deemed appropriate during the planning phase) might not be a bad move, since a compliance and ethics program can be very information intensive.

Management should not be developing processes, procedures, reports, and so forth during the audit. Rather, the audit team should be evaluating the efforts of the compliance and ethics program in meeting the organization's needs. Finally, management should complete a self-assessment prior to an internal audit, and study various pieces of guidance, such as the OCEG guide for the audit of a compliance and ethics program.

Establishing accountability for your anti-fraud efforts

Some companies have far lower levels of misappropriation of assets and fraudulent financial reporting than others. Why? Because they aggressively take steps to prevent and detect fraud, end of story. At these exemplary companies, *management* takes seriously its ethical responsibilities for designing and implementing systems, procedures and controls to catch fraud – and, along with the Board of Directors, for promoting a culture and corporate environment that demands honesty and ethical behavior. How does your company stack up?

Run through this short checklist:

- Does your organization have a strong fraud oversight process at both the Board and management levels?

- Does your organization have robust and effective anti-fraud policies, procedures and controls?
- Does management regularly evaluate fraud risks and anti-fraud controls?
- Have the risks of management override and conflicts of interest been independently reviewed within the last 12 months?
- Would you say your workforce has a strong ethical culture?
- Does your company have a corporate policy that encourages whistleblowers to come forward, and do those would be whistleblowers actually believe it?

If you answered "yes" to all of the above questions, great. You're well on your way to a strong anti-fraud effort. Now answer three more questions that will help you get ahead of the crowd:

1 What are the Board's and management's roles regarding fraud?
2 What should the internal audit team's role be regarding fraud?
3 How can the organization best help the external auditor meet its responsibilities for evaluating fraud risks?

To answer that last question properly, you need clear answers to two questions immediately preceding it. Specifically: The Board is responsible for defining and approving the organization's overall strategic direction and system of internal control, as well as for setting the tone at the top (overall corporate governance). Management operates the business within the guidelines set by the Board, periodically reporting on performance and progress toward key strategies and objectives. Management also monitors operations. That includes regular assessments of the effectiveness of the overall system of internal control against the requirements set by the Board, as well as the company's own ethical values and beliefs.

As mentioned earlier, the Board is accountable for ensuring that an effective system of internal control is *established* to fight fraud; management is responsible for how that system is *designed and enforced* to fight fraud. Once you have that clear – and actually done – the internal audit department can also contribute to those anti-fraud efforts.

Audit's job: helping fraud prevention efforts

Today there is the belief that auditors are looking for – as well as investigating and stopping – frauds. After all, aren't auditors the last line of defense in identifying crooked management? Well, no. The truth is that nobody can catch all fraud, and the internal audit department should address the misperception that this is internal auditing's purpose.

Everyone in the company has a role in fraud prevention and detection, and the primary responsibility lies with all members of management (and by that, I mean managers at every level of the company).

An effective internal audit function improves the company's ethical culture and control environment, both overtly through its audit work and in a more general sense by promoting good practices. Internal audits of anti-fraud activities provide valuable feedback to management and the Board on where they can improve overall performance, which contributes in the long term to more effective fraud-risk management efforts. It can also be a deterrent when employees know that the internal audit department employs persons with fraud detection knowledge, skills and tools.

Internal audit should design and plan audits specifically to detect fraud, which directly strengthens the organization's internal control system. The internal audit plan should be driven by an audit risk assessment (that is, the risk that an audit might miss something); likewise, efforts against fraud should be driven by a fraud risk assessment, because the greater the organization's exposure to fraud, the more anti-fraud audit effort must be allocated. Moreover, you must conduct fraud risk assessments thoughtfully, since it does not help to have your workforce believing the internal audit team distrusts everybody.

Audit work should include evaluating the organization's efforts in fraud prevention, fraud detection and fraud investigation. If "detective" procedures are not in place, frauds that are discovered will require more investigative effort and result in greater loss. Over the long term, fraud *prevention* and *deterrence* efforts have the most impact on reducing fraud, so this should be a top management priority *and* be regularly evaluated by internal audit.

Always remember that auditing provides only a *reasonable* level of assurance; auditors cannot, and will not, provide an insurance policy against every possible fraud. However, because of their objectivity and integrity, internal auditors are able to reinforce an organization's anti-fraud effort by investigating reports of possible fraudulent behavior. In fact, more and more corporate internal audit departments include trained forensic accountants.

There are numerous fraud audit techniques today, and more should be incorporated into audit departments. Some simple examples of forensic exercises include: correlating employee names, addresses and other contact details against the supplier database to help identify suspect transactions; examining expenses claims closely; following up religiously on seemingly insignificant discrepancies in control totals; using data mining and computer audit techniques in general to craft and answer cunning questions; and always being aware of the possibility of collusion, deception and fraud.

Some useful anti-fraud management practices include:

- **Practice 1**: Identifying potential indicators of fraud for your industry, company or activities within your organization.
- **Practice 2**: Communicating with experienced people to learn ideas about how frauds may be committed and best detected.
- **Practice 3**: Devising and routinely running tests to look for fraud indicators and data anomalies.
- **Practice 4**: Performing *ad-hoc* inquiries as needed to dig into the source data underlying fraud indicators and data anomalies; and perform or include as part of control self-assessment sessions.
- **Practice 5**: Implementing continuous auditing.

Norman Marks, a chief internal audit executive at BusinessObjects and old hand at internal auditing at large companies, recommends that internal audit periodically assess:

- The adequacy of the control environment, including: the adequacy of the Code of Conduct and processes to ensure it is understood, the adequacy of the whistleblower and investigation processes, and the staffing and organization of those responsible for the prevention and detection of fraud. Internal audit should go beyond traditional techniques, such as interviewing or issuing a questionnaire only to senior management; a direct and more useful technique is to ask the workforce via surveys, interviews and focus groups.

- Management's risk assessment as it relates to fraud and theft, including whether: the process is systematic and most conceivable fraud schemes are identified, fraud risks are adequately assessed and appropriate strategies implemented.
- Management's monitoring activities, including: whether actual losses are monitored and compared to risk tolerances, and whether actual losses are monitored to identify areas of concern, potential failing of controls and opportunities for improvement.

There will always be limits to an organization's anti-fraud capabilities. Sample sizes can only be so large. A budget is only so big. Fraudsters, meanwhile, are cunning people who work hard to conceal their activities and exploit weaknesses in controls.

Organizations must be ever diligent

An open discussion about the possibility of fraud (of serious fraud), and the necessary responses, is always vital. Ideally, your company should have that discussion before a serious fraud incident, rather than afterward. If you want confirmation of that, look at Société Générale reeling from the multibillion-dollar fraud committed by one person. Now is not the best time for SG to ask how such a thing could happen.

Setting clear expectations and defining everyone's responsibilities regarding your anti-fraud efforts is half the battle. Being diligent in your efforts is the other half. To fight fraud, we need a firm policy, it must be enforced, and violators must be investigated and appropriate actions taken. Management must understand that it has the responsibility to design and implement anti-fraud activities, including the monitoring of the results. Internal auditors should also search for fraudulent activities and contribute to the organization's "no tolerance" attitude toward fraud.

Once your own house is in order, also consider the potential fraud risks relating to your key business relationships. Whistle blowing by suppliers, partners, or customers is one of the most common ways of discovering fraudulent activities, and it cuts both ways. If a worker at one of your business partner companies wanted to report fraud at your company, would that person have the means (and the encouragement) to do so? What if one of your employees discovered fraud happening at one of your partners? How would you deal with it?

Auditing to spot fraud, from start to end

The Sarbanes-Oxley Act was enacted to help fight corporate fraud. Public companies have spent untold millions to comply and hired compliance and ethics officers ostensibly to ensure that the law is adhered to. Yet, somehow, at the end of the day, fraud is still here. However comprehensive your code of ethics may be, and however many policies you have, realize this one truth: Your organization could be the next one to hit the headlines. Simply saying, "We strive for the highest ethical standards in our business," and passing that off as your "tone at the top" will never deter a morally challenged insider from ripping you off. Insider fraud is always a threat, and a company must always police against it. Once you

2: The Professional Practice of Internal Audit

understand that, it's just a matter of a modest investment of financial and human resources to implement and enforce policies and procedures with teeth.

Establishing a robust anti-fraud program

Fraud can range from minor staff theft to misappropriation of assets and fraudulent financial reporting. It also can include embezzlement, identity theft, vendor fraud, conspiracy and theft of proprietary information. Material financial-statement fraud also can wreak havoc on an organization's market value, reputation and ability to achieve its strategic objectives.

The risk of fraud can be reduced through a combination of prevention, deterrence and detection measures. Organizations need to adopt tough anti-fraud policies, strong internal controls, accountability on the part of all managers, training of employees in fraud awareness, liaison with law enforcement, and other "brass tacks" measures. Consider putting on the management committee's monthly agenda a standing discussion of what the organization is doing to reduce the occurrence of fraud, and schedule a formal internal audit of the organization's anti-fraud program each year.

Evaluate anti-fraud controls regularly

Establishing an anti-fraud program is one thing, but there is nothing worse than having a policy that nobody follows. Identifying and measuring fraud risk is one of the first steps in implementing a robust anti-fraud program. Certain fraud risks also can be reduced by making improvements to the organization's policies, procedures, or processes, and fraud-risk assessments and fraud-risk management efforts contribute to the improvement effort.

Periodically conducting an internal audit of the anti-fraud program is very productive as an independent and objective assessment of current policies and practices. To do this, first conduct the fraud-risk assessment, then identify the key fraud controls and any control gaps, and finally test the effectiveness of the controls. Continuous monitoring by management and continuous auditing by the auditors are also very effective in tackling fraud directly. Many organizations are establishing continuous monitoring and continuous auditing efforts for their critical transactions and information systems – you should, too.

Risk of management override

Yet another fraud risk threatens to undermine all of these efforts that have been discussed thus far: management override. A company can have stellar procedures to block fraud, but they won't do much good if the top brass simply allows some improper transaction to circumvent those procedures. Consider having the internal audit department independently review the month- and year-end accounting activities for any unusual transactions, such as suspect journal entries or reversals. The control owner might also be assigned this important task. You also should consider having an open debate at the audit-committee meeting on what the committee and the company itself are doing to reduce the risk of management override.

An appropriate oversight process

The audit committee should evaluate management's identification of fraud risks, implementation of anti-fraud measures, and creation of an appropriate "tone at the top." Active oversight by the audit committee also will help reinforce management's commitment to creating zero tolerance for fraud. The audit committee plays a critical role in helping the Board of Directors fulfill its oversight responsibilities for financial reporting and other governance activities. To assess risks of things like forgery, credit-card fraud, conspiracy, computer sabotage, Internet-based fraud, and so forth, the organization and the audit committee should consider obtaining the advice of specialists, using internal or contracted resources to compile detailed reports regarding vulnerabilities and recommend fraud exposure-reducing actions.

The audit committee also needs to beware of enterprise-threatening fraud risks. While management must cover the entire spectrum of fraud risks, the Board needs to be focused on the significant fraud risks and ensuring that an effective risk management strategy and supporting processes have been implemented. Having an ongoing debate about what the oversight process should be is a good thing, and evaluation of its effectiveness is even better. The parties contributing to oversight efforts include the Board, senior management, the internal auditors, the external auditors and (on occasions) certified fraud examiners. Knowing who is responsible for what, and when to lean on their expertise, will ensure a winning team effort.

Creating an ethical culture

The company is responsible for creating a culture of honesty and strong ethics and for communicating clearly the acceptable behavior and expectations of each employee. Directors and officers of the organization set the tone at the top for ethical behavior within the organization. Employees should be given the opportunity to obtain advice internally before making decisions that could have significant legal or ethical implications. They also should be encouraged and given the ability to communicate about potential violations of the entity's Code of Conduct, anonymously if need be (such as via a confidential hotline service).

The Open Compliance and Ethics Group's *Hotline & Helpline Handbook* provides a wealth of guidance for implementing this important fraud reduction measure. It has been proven that the ability for staff to safely report issues will reduce the incidence and impact of fraud.

We also need to make managers more accountable for their operations, that is, we should not be waiting for audits to make changes. Management is responsible for the organization's system of internal control, and the effectiveness of its operation, and I strongly encourage managers to evaluate their own results. (It's called operational monitoring and process improvement.)

Be diligent

An open discussion among the key stakeholders, and ideally prior to any front-page news, is always recommended. Setting clear expectations for everyone involved (regarding your anti-fraud efforts) is half the battle. Being diligent in your efforts is the other half. To truly fight fraud, we need a firm policy that must be enforced, and violators must be investigated and action taken. Fraud-risk management is here to stay – has your organization implemented an effective strategy for fraud prevention, detection and response? At the end of the day, are you part of the problem or part of the solution?

CHAPTER 3: IMPROVING INTERNAL AUDIT RESULTS

Quality is such an attractive banner that sometimes we think we can get away with just waving it, without doing the hard work necessary to achieve it.

Miles Maguire

The vital need for quality internal auditing

In the past few years, massive efforts have been expended to prepare and implement the requirements of the Sarbanes-Oxley Act, in particular, Section 404(b). While a corporation's management and board of directors have always been responsible for internal control, the level of scrutiny by the investing public and the regulatory bodies has reached new levels. As a result, today, more than ever before, an organization's internal audit function must be robust and contribute to ensuring the accuracy of financial reporting. There's no question that fostering a strong internal audit department should be a high priority for management. Indeed, the Institute for Internal Auditors spells out as much in its *International Standards for the Professional Practice of Internal Auditing*:

The chief audit executive should develop and maintain a quality assurance and improvement program that covers all aspects of the internal audit activity and continuously monitors its effectiveness.

Fundamentally, internal audit efforts are focused on identifying the key goals, issues and challenges facing an organization and evaluating its progress. Internal auditors also assess senior management's procedures and related controls for achieving those objectives, while identifying opportunities for improvement. Each organization has different goals and objectives, and certainly specific issues and challenges facing a company depend on the business environment involved. Therefore, unfortunately, there is no one-size-fits-all internal audit process, nor one audit approach that fits all situations. However, companies can ask themselves a few basic questions about what sort of internal audit function they want, and take steps to ensure the internal auditing they do meets those expectations. Start by defining the function. Internal audit provides strategic, operational and tactical value to an organization's operations. For example, internal auditing is:

- a resource to the Board and management for ensuring the entire organization has the resources, systems and processes for operating an efficient and effective operation
- an assurance tool for management and the Board to know all that should be done is being done – by ensuring qualified professional reviews and tests are performed, the Board and management can advance the goal of overseeing the organization's operations and ensuring its continuous improvement and success.
- an independent validation that the organization's efforts are proactive and effective against current and emerging threats.

Some key questions the audit committee should be asking management:

- Has a quality assurance and improvement program within internal audit been established? What are the results to date?

- How do we know the internal audit function is effective? What are the key performance measures and results to date?
- How is the internal audit function doing in relation to the *International Standards for the Professional Practice of Internal Auditing*? What are the strengths and weaknesses?
- Has the internal audit department begun its journey in quality?

Enter quality assurance

Professionalism does not occur overnight; it takes time. Professionalism evolves from dedication, professional growth and staff effort. Integral to this process – and the essence of excellence in the business environment – is quality.

To ensure consistent quality in your internal audit function, a quality assurance and improvement program is necessary. The required elements include ongoing and periodic internal quality assessments, external quality assessments, internal monitoring, and assurance that the internal audit activity is complying with the relevant Standards and the Code of Ethics. An external quality assessment, or QA, evaluates compliance with the Standards, the internal audit and audit committee charters, the organization's risk and control assessment, and the use of best practices.

Regardless of an organization's industry or the internal audit team's complexity or size, two approved approaches to external QA are at the company's disposal. The first approach, an external assessment with independent validation, involves an outside team under the leadership of an experienced and professional project manager. The team members should be competent professionals who are well versed in best internal audit practices.

The second approach seeks out an objective outside party for independent validation of an internal self-assessment and report completed by the internal audit group. This approach brings in a competent, independent evaluator experienced in quality assessment methodology to validate the aforementioned self-assessment of the internal audit activity. In addition to reviewing the self-assessment, the evaluator substantiates some of the work done by the self-assessment team, makes an on-site visit, interviews senior management, and either co-signs the chief audit executive's report regarding conformity to the Standards or issues a separate report on the disparities.

The external quality assessment provides the audit committee and management with an official "report card" on the internal audit department's efforts and identifies opportunities for improvement. An effective internal audit function understands the organization, its culture, operations and risk profile. This makes audit a valuable resource for management, the Board and its designated audit committee. The objectivity, skills and knowledge of competent internal auditors can significantly add value to an organization's internal control, risk management and governance processes. Similarly, effective internal audit can provide assurance to other stakeholders, such as regulators, employees, investors, external auditors and shareholders. Completing the external quality assessment provides assurance to the audit committee and the Board that internal audit is doing all the things it should be doing. Moreover, in today's climate of enhanced attention to financial reporting – a climate not likely to change any time soon – that robust internal audit function can only strengthen corporate performance.

Enhancing your internal audit performance

The internal audit function's position within a company is unique. It provides its principal stakeholders (audit committee members and management) with valuable and objective assurance on governance, risk management and control processes, as well as consulting services to improve operations. With this critical responsibility to fulfill it is expected that internal audit will continuously improve its own practices. How do you do that?

A high-quality internal audit function meets or exceeds stakeholder expectations, while ensuring that value is added to the organization. The most critical factor in achieving internal audit quality is the auditor's competency and proficiency in evaluating the organization's risk management, control and governance processes. Each internal audit department should have a program, not only to ensure top quality internal audit reports, investigations, consulting and other services, but it should also have a way to effect continuous improvement in its service to stakeholders.

Steps to success

The Institute of Internal Auditors (IIA) has issued a "quality maturity model" that includes a roadmap for improving internal audit practices over time. The model comprises five basic levels:

- **Level 1: Introductory**. The internal audit function at this level has no quality assurance and improvement program in place. Typically, a Level 1 internal audit department would be fairly new or one that has not yet conformed to the quality requirements within the IIA's *International Standards for the Professional Practice of Internal Audit*. In other cases, the chief auditing executive or the audit committee lacks a clear understanding of the substantial value that such a program can bring to an organization.
- **Level 2: Emerging**. The internal audit function conducts periodic and ongoing self-assessments, or internal quality assessments, monitoring the department's compliance with the Standards.
- **Level 3: Established**. The internal audit activity obtains an independent evaluation of its self-assessment and improvement efforts at least every five years.
- **Level 4: Progressive**. A quality assurance and improvement program is integrated into the operations of the internal audit activity. The activity generally complies with the Standards and Code of Ethics, and obtains an external quality assurance review at least every five years.
- **Level 5: Advanced**. An active and fully integrated quality assurance and improvement program exists within the daily operations of the internal audit function. An external QA is conducted at least every three years. All staff members follow a rigorous continuing education program.

In most enterprises, the audit committee oversees the internal audit function. As such, audit committee members should have direct interaction with the leadership and activities of the internal audit team and should monitor the internal audit team's performance. Using the quality maturity model's guidance to discuss regularly the internal audit department's continuous improvement efforts will encourage a world-class audit function. Regular revisiting of internal audit department's quality "progress" will also influence the motivation and focus of the audit team.

Other board guidance

The IIA's briefing paper, *Internal Audit Standards: Why They Matter*, presents a series of questions to facilitate a closer relationship between the audit committee and internal auditing.

This guidance also provides a summary of typical audit-committee oversight responsibilities. Directors of enterprises that have internal audit departments are expected to determine whether the internal audit function works effectively. Where an internal audit function has not been formally established, these questions should be discussed with senior management. The IIA has also issued the landmark board-level guidance, *20 Questions Directors Should Ask About Internal Audit*, to help audit committees develop a better understanding of, and establish performance standards for, the chief auditing executive's activities.

The first important area to explore is the mandate of the internal audit function, including what services it should provide and what its priorities should be. Ask yourself: Is internal audit focused on the right things? For example, does the internal audit function evaluate the company's efforts to establish an effective enterprise-wide risk management program?

Another important topic is the audit committee's relationship with the internal audit function. Here, the key issues are whether the internal audit activities are supported by the audit committee (for example, ensuring appropriate prominence on the organizational chart) and what influence management has on the internal audit function through its organizational structure. Are there open lines of communication between the chair of the audit committee and the chief audit executive? Is there an executive session with the chief audit executive (CAE) at every audit committee meeting to ensure frank discussion?

A third concern is resources. Does internal audit have the appropriate level of resources with the right skill sets to produce desired results? If not, auditing of the business and the depth of analysis can be inappropriate. Internal audit requires highly skilled resources, and the competition for staff becomes more difficult each year. A long-term workforce plan would be very beneficial in today's complex and fast-changing business environment. An annual audit committee's review of the internal audit function *and* enterprise-wide human resource planning can be invaluable.

Finally, the results of the internal audit efforts should be reviewed regularly by the audit committee, and an overall determination made about whether the audit committee is satisfied with the information and performance it receives from internal auditing.

Adopting excellence

Confirming that your internal audit function is on the road to quality – and consequently helping to ensure the ongoing value of your internal audit activity – will bring great benefits to your organization and its stakeholders. A few steps CAEs should consider taking:

- **Step 1**: Educate themselves and their staff in quality practices.
- **Step 2**: Define their stakeholders: shareholders, the audit committee, executives, corporate management and business unit managers, at the least; perhaps more for your specific enterprise.
- **Step 3**: Brainstorm with staff. Let them tell you what they see as their collective strengths and weaknesses. What do they need and what do they desire to become more effective and productive?
- **Step 4**: Involve stakeholders in an initial conversation about expectations and needs; conduct brainstorming sessions and determine what you do well and what areas need improvement.
- **Step 5**: Create, distribute and tabulate a survey for your various levels, and implement change improvements.
- **Step 6**: Periodically review your progress, and determine where additional change and improvement is needed.
- **Step 7**: Continue to track those areas where you can be most effective. Publish your accomplishments and improvements.
- **Step 8**: Engage outside fraud investigators to teach internal auditors what to look for, and have them work with auditors on internal cases to help auditors appreciate what they are looking for and how insiders try to hide those things. Consider the use of other outside specialists as department needs dictate.

The audit committee, meanwhile, has some questions of its own that it should be asking:

- Has a quality assurance and improvement program within internal audit been established? What are the results to date?
- How do we know the internal audit function is effective? What are the key performance measures and results to date? How many errors and/or frauds have been detected through audits per year? Are the rates of detection changing from year to year, and why or why not?
- What kind of control weaknesses, revenue gains, or expense reductions have been identified? Is internal audit making an impact?
- How is the internal audit function doing in relation to the *International Standards for the Professional Practice of Internal Auditing*? What are the strengths and weaknesses of the internal audit department?

Is your organization's internal audit function practicing what it preaches? That is, has internal audit established a long-term continuous improvement program? Finally, is the audit committee doing all it can to ensure the internal audit function has the organizational status, independence, and objectivity to complete its mandate effectively?

The bottom line is that improving the internal audit department's performance will help improve the whole enterprise's performance as well. That is, effective internal auditing can be leveraged across the company. The audit committee must provide effective oversight over internal audit. By using the right guidance and by asking the right questions, it can do just that.

The art of expressing an internal audit opinion

Executive management, audit committees and the Board want to know whether their internal control systems work. The chief audit executive is often requested to issue an opinion on the adequacy of internal controls within the organization to meet this assurance need. If a CAE does issue a formal opinion, it is crucial that all parties clearly understand the areas and issues the CAE is addressing in doing so. Otherwise, brace yourself for expectation gaps.

Expressing opinions is no easy task. The CAE must consider the scope of the audit effort and the nature and extent of auditing performed, and evaluate what the evidence from the audit(s) says about the adequacy of internal controls. A formal audit opinion should clearly express four points:

- the evaluation criteria and structure used
- the scope over which the opinion applies
- who has responsibility to establish and maintain the system of internal control
- the specific type of opinion being expressed.

Extensive planning to express an opinion

In planning the opinion, internal audit needs to understand the current "maturity" of the internal audit efforts and where the organization is in its efforts to implement a robust system of internal control. Some key questions to consider include:

- Has the internal audit function evaluated the system of internal control previously?

- How well documented, stable and understood are the organization's controls? (Expressing an opinion is much easier in an organization where statements and management assertions about internal controls already exist, since the auditors can examine the processes underlying the statements and assertions to form their opinion.)
- Has this evaluation been discussed with the Board of Directors?
- How accurate is the disclosure to your shareholders and other stakeholders?
- Have there been adverse opinions by the external auditor?

In addition to the maturity of the internal audit effort and maturity of the organization's system of internal control, a third dimension must also be considered. That is, at what level of internal control is an internal audit opinion required? The initial SOX-initiated internal control evaluations often covered thousands of controls, which took an inordinate amount of audit time and resources. A lesson learned was to scale back and be more selective regarding the controls to be evaluated. This is a crucial scoping decision; rather than jumping into an examination of a vast number of controls, a SOX lesson has been to focus on the "key" controls. In practice, the burning question now is, exactly which are the key controls? This can only be answered in reference to the purpose being served by the internal audit opinion. What do the users of that opinion want and need?

The audit department has to consider the reality that an organization with evolving internal controls will need considerably more time and effort to identify, test and assess controls than one with stable and well-understood controls. It may also make a difference in the caveats that should be placed on the internal audit opinion. In fact, an important message has been that depending on your starting point – especially for many internal audit shops not yet providing an opinion at the "organizational" level – it will take multiple years before you have enough work and knowledge to provide an overall opinion. The issue of gathering sufficient information from all significant areas of an organization – compliance, disaster recovery, environmental, risk management, governance and internal control – to form an overall opinion is very daunting (read: amazingly labor intensive).

Communicating the results

Assuming planning was effective, expectations were clearly set, and audit testing was sufficient to support an opinion of some type, when internal audit communicates its opinion on the system of internal control there is still much to consider in issuing the actual opinion, including:

- **The evaluation criteria used must be clearly stated**: **(what control model was used to complete the opinion, or even just what standards were used to form the opinion).** Complications always exist. For example, the COSO model is most often used to evaluate the overall system of internal control, while the COBIT model is commonly used for general IT controls. The internal-audit and the IT audit efforts both need to contribute to the overall audit opinion regarding the system of internal control.

- **The scope over which the opinion applies must be clearly communicated in the opinions document**. What areas of the organization are covered, what work was completed, and what period is involved, are all examples of the details that need to be covered within the scope statement. An opinion with a well-defined scope will not leave the reader guessing as to the relevance and focus of the opinion, nor the time period to which it applies.
- **Clear responsibility for the establishment and maintenance of internal controls**. Here the issue is ensuring that management's responsibility for internal controls and the Board's oversight regarding the system of internal control are both clearly stated. Internal audit is to provide assurances regarding the performance of controls and the system of internal control, but it should not take on any management responsibilities for internal control.
- **The specific type of opinion being expressed by the auditor**. There are varying levels of assurance possible regarding internal control opinions, as well as both positive and negative assurance opinions. Fundamentally, negative assurance indicates nothing came to the attention of the auditor during the audit, while positive assurance indicates the auditor has performed sufficient testing, so that the auditor believes it is very unlikely that anything materially wrong is occurring. Here, the issue is audit workload; more assurance means more work. In addition, while the CEO and CFO can certify that their financial statements and the processes to create them are accurate, the senior executives are responsible for these processes. Internal audit needs to complete enough audit work to provide

sufficient support for its opinion, which is something quite different.

- **Other considerations**. There are always other issues to consider and usually these are situation-specific. Be forewarned that expressing an opinion on the system of internal control is complicated and a long-term proposition. Also, like so many other complicated things, about the third time you've completed it, it'll finally fall into place.

The assurance needs of the audit committee and management are very similar, but they do differ. For example, fundamentally the Board wants to know that the overall system of internal control is robust and working effectively and reliably. While this is important to management, executives also want to know what significant improvement opportunities exist, and how they can make the organization more cost effective. Internal audit needs to balance the assurance needs of both these audiences, and deliver on both.

An extensive discussion between all the key parties up front is crucial, as the setting of clear expectations and overall goals is absolutely required. As the old expression goes: "Plan your work, and work your plan." This definitely applies to audit opinions.

Driving internal audit with risk assessments

For an internal audit function to be effective, its efforts must be risk based and must meet the organization's long-term assurance requirements. Members of the Board, the audit committee and executive management look to internal audit to cover the entire spectrum of risks and issues facing the organization; that is, they expect internal audit to assess the significant risks to the organization and provide timely assurance that adequate controls are operating effectively to mitigate those risks. It is a huge responsibility. Most organizations have numerous potentially auditable entities (corporate initiatives, business lines, systems, regulatory requirements; the list is endless) and internal audit must decide which of these entities they are going to tackle first. The audit risk assessment works to bring at least a semblance of order to the audit universe, evaluating the various possibilities and attempting to address the potential risks facing the organization.

Risk assessments and auditing priorities

The *International Standards for the Professional Practice of Internal Auditing*, as promulgated by the Institute of Internal Auditors, specify that:

- The chief audit executive should establish risk-based plans to determine the priorities of the internal audit activity, consistent with the organization's goals (Standard No. 2010 – Planning).
- The internal audit activity's plan of engagements should be based on a risk assessment undertaken at least annually. The input of senior management and the Board should be considered in this process (Standard No. 2010A). That is to say, internal audit plans and priorities must be driven by a risk assessment at both the macro level (for the annual plan) and the micro level (for each audit engagement).

Audit risk assessments come in all shapes and sizes, reflecting the vast diversity of business environments: from very formal, very detailed, annual assessments, to more of a rolling high-level analysis on a quarterly or even monthly basis (even moving to an almost continuous basis for some organizations) with the related audit plans being revised almost as regularly.

To develop an audit plan, the risk assessment evaluates the key forces that create risk for the organization and assesses two fundamental factors:

- the potential impact of a risk's occurrence
- the likelihood of that occurrence.

Those factors must also be aligned with the business environment in which the organization operates; in other words, they must be relevant. The audit risk assessment is not an end – it is a means to an end. Internal audit needs to define the audit universe and assess the risks facing the organization in achieving its objectives, so that audit efforts can be properly prioritized.

Revisiting the risk assessment regularly helps ensure that the path you take continues to be the right one. After all, mid-course corrections are always needed. Consider a plane flying from New York to San Francisco. A flight plan is created based on all the factors known prior to leaving New York – which is to say, the risks and requirements are assessed (weather concerns, traffic issues, equipment capabilities, and so forth). Throughout the flight, progress is monitored and mid-flight corrections are made to ensure the flight is efficient and on the right path. Finally, upon arrival, a post-trip evaluation is completed to determine what, if anything, should be changed for the next trip.

Now apply that approach to the world of corporate auditing. What priority should be assigned to an audit of, say, the human resources department's efforts, versus the security system for an organization's numerous inventory warehouses? If the skills and creativity of the organization's workforce truly drive the long-term success of the organization, HR might be the logical target for your next big audit. Conversely, if the products in the warehouse (if compromised) could bring the organization to its knees, then a security audit might be the top priority.

In other words, improving the risk assessment process helps to ensure that audit priorities are appropriate. Moreover, what if your audit risk assessment is wrong? My answer has always been that it's better to try to forecast the future than just to let it happen to you. Besides, whenever you have analysis and debate about risks – their potential to disrupt, the controls and contingency plans to address them, and so forth – that invariably strengthens the organization. It's just human nature: if you give the auditor and management a flashlight and tell them to look in their closets each year, eventually people start cleaning those closets up.

The internal audit plan is a "roadmap"

The end result of the risk assessment process is the internal audit plan. Establishing or updating an internal audit plan isn't always easy, but it is critical; without a plan you are not in control. Without an approved plan you also don't have the needed support and (equally important) agreement on what the long-term assurance requirements for the organization truly are. An important issue in developing the internal audit plan is the involvement of management. While the input from management stakeholders is vital, the independent judgment and final decisions need to rest mainly with the chief audit executive. Management cannot dictate audit priorities.

In an established audit function, with many years of experience with audit plans, a meeting with a few executive guests can complete the review and provide a final proposal to the audit committee. At the end of the day, the audit committee (representing the Board's many interests) is responsible for approving the CAE's audit plan. Presenting the proposed internal audit plan to the audit committee for approval is one of the most critical activities within internal audit. The audit committee's stamp of approval sets the direction for internal audit's efforts, and facilitates senior executives' debates about:

- what is really important to the company
- what challenges are facing the company
- what the internal audit department believes to be the key risks facing the company.

As corporate governance debates go, they don't get any better than that! Directors must satisfy themselves that the audit plans are appropriate and that internal audit will contribute to the organization's performance results. The dialogue between management, the audit committee, and the chief audit executive regarding the audit plan ensures that internal audit has a seat at the governance table. In general, development of an effective audit plan involves a combination of everything written herein: risk assessment, dialogue among all the key stakeholders, a consensus on what internal audit wants to achieve, and finally, what assurance needs for the organization must be met.

Finally, an approved audit plan is not the end of implementing an effective internal audit function; it's more like the beginning of a new year, and very similar to the approval of the organization's annual budget – where you've decided what the priorities are, what you're going to spend, where you plan to spend it, and what you expect to get. Nonetheless, throughout the year you'll still need to assess changes to the risk profiles and the related plan, propose adjustments to the audit committee, and most importantly, meet your many goals and objectives.

Giving internal audit an effective mandate

Internal auditing's unique position within a company provides management and audit committee members with valuable assistance, by giving objective assurance on governance, risk management and control processes. For internal audit to be effective, however, the mandate of the internal audit function must be clearly defined, agreed to by all stakeholders, and approved by the Board. Executive management and members of the audit committee are the two key stakeholders in most organizations, so involving them is critical to ensure the internal audit mandate is balanced and meets the needs of everyone in the company. Also, remember that resourcing is driven by the mandate; that is, an incomplete mandate will lead to inappropriate allocation of resources.

The mandate: a critical success factor

The authority of the internal audit department is documented in its internal audit charter. An important area to explore first is the role the internal audit department should have: What services should it provide? What should its priorities be? Discussions with members of the audit committee and management should be held to determine what assurance and consulting services are needed. Exploring what internal audit departments at peer companies are doing can also be useful, and helps ensure that the approved internal audit mandate is current with best audit practice.

The internal audit department must support the audit committee's responsibilities, so the committee's charter should be reviewed when defining internal auditing's roles and responsibilities. In fact, an annual "alignment review" of the two charters – audit committee and internal audit – is strongly recommended. While the NYSE listing rules require an annual review of the audit committee's mandate, it is silent regarding internal audit. In my view, reviewing both charters every year makes good business sense, and the internal audit charter and the audit committee charter should be mutually supportive and reinforce their critical relationship.

Tackling the internal audit charter

Establishing or updating an internal audit charter isn't always easy. A variety of components need to be developed, and usually a company must go through several iterations of the charter's actual content before striking the right tone. Participation by the entire internal audit department staff – at least the management team of internal audit – is crucial; without involvement, after all, there's no commitment.

The overall mission and scope of work should be defined first; one good place to start is an accountability statement for the chief audit executive. Companies should also discuss issues of independence, for example, who sets the scope of internal audit projects, and to whom should the chief auditing executive report? (Another quick tip: including a statement in the charter about the auditor's open and free access to all information across the organization can save your auditors a lot of grief.)

The responsibilities of the department – what the function is and is not accountable for – comprise the majority of an internal audit charter. Inclusion of a standard of performance is also common to delineate what standards should be used by the internal audit function in the performance of its work. The most common standard is the *International Standards for the Professional Practice of Internal Auditing*, as promulgated by the Institute of Internal Auditors.

Once a draft internal audit charter has been developed or updated, it needs to be reviewed by the stakeholder groups, and there are many different ways to get a draft charter approved and published. One common approach is to set aside time during an off-site meeting of internal audit staffers and management – with key executives like the CEO and CFO visiting – for the review and finalization of the audit charter. With web-based interactive technology, the virtual sharing of the draft charter with all the stakeholders has become very popular, as it enables open-threaded discussions to take their course, and can increase acceptance levels. At smaller companies, a few key executives at a single staff meeting can finish the document in a morning. Development of an effective audit charter generally involves a combination of all of the above methods, plus others.

Revisit the mandate annually

The mandate of the internal audit department – defined in the internal audit charter – assists the department in performing its work because management and others are able to understand clearly what internal audit is charged with doing, and what they are accountable for. The audit charter is also a great communication vehicle for internal audit to discuss its services and priorities with clients and stakeholders. In top-tier organizations that take governance seriously, presenting the approved internal audit mandate to the Board or management committee is a common way of presenting the future: the goals of internal audit, the value the function brings to the organization, and its priorities and plans. This is also an excellent way for internal audit to obtain management's agreement and feedback on the internal audit plans.

Directors must satisfy themselves that the mandate of internal audit is appropriate and that the internal audit function will contribute to the organization's efforts. The dialogue between management, the audit committee, and the leadership of the internal audit function regarding the mandate is one of the keys to an internal auditing department's long-term success.

An approved and published internal audit charter is not the end of implementing an effective internal audit function; it's more like the end of the beginning. Really, the audit mandate is revisited with every new audit project as employees ask: "Why are we doing this?" Having a clear, approved charter makes answering that question much easier.

The value of "performance measurement"

Steven Covey, author of *The Seven Habits of Highly Effective People*, and many others, quite rightly recommend that when you start any kind of new project, you should begin with the end in mind. What does that involve?

- deciding where you want to be in the future (that is, what your "end state" will be)
- defining your key goals and objectives in getting there (to guide your various efforts along the way)
- building and then implementing your plan to get there (the means to reach your desired end state).

This planning cycle works for all individuals, in both their professional and personal lives. It is even more important for organizations, where an understanding across the whole enterprise is vital in obtaining broad support across a workforce faced with numerous, and many times conflicting, priorities. For internal auditors this planning cycle takes on a special meaning as well. Successful auditing requires an understanding of what the organization is trying to achieve and factoring that understanding into the company's auditing efforts. As an important activity itself, internal audit needs to define what the audit team is trying to achieve; without doing that, the auditing team may end up going down a wrong road during its project. For the organization to understand what the audit team is trying to achieve, the audit team itself must understand and communicate what it wants to accomplish.

The bottom line: auditors should be:

- encouraging and verifying that organizations have robust systems to measure and report performance
- leveraging the information from such systems in planning their audit efforts
- walking the line themselves, by defining their long-term goals, the means to get there, and reporting their progress to the audit committee.

As part of tracking the audit's progress, periodic measurement and reporting is vital, and serves as a bridge between today's work and tomorrow's. Put another way, an audit team must define its road map, get agreement with all the stakeholders that the path is correct (including the auditing project's goals, the plan and proposed end state), and then monitor and report progress in getting there. A robust performance measurement and reporting program facilitates the ongoing monitoring of progress, the regular (and sometimes painful) debate of issues and interim results along the way, and the corrective actions and adjustments necessary to remain headed where you need to go.

All of the above concepts apply at the various levels of the organization, from the enterprise as a whole down to subsidiaries and significant business units. As the internal auditing team evaluates various aspects of the organization, each audit should consider in its evaluation whether performance measurement and reporting is contributing to the setting of direction and the execution of plans.

The art of measurement

A well-known maxim is, "What gets measured gets done." All enterprise processes, including an audit, can benefit from measurement. Ideally, measurement will help an organization:

- show how these results support organizational objectives
- determine what works and what doesn't
- justify capital allocation
- motivate and provide tangible feedback to employees
- enhance the ability to communicate with stakeholders.

A critical element of performance measurement is establishing key performance indicators and metrics. In terms of metrics, they need to be "SMART," i.e. Specific, Measurable, Actionable, Relevant and Timely. Another important consideration is not to overload the process with too many metrics, but to focus on those most relevant to assuring the organization is creating shareholder value. (One excellent reference guide is the Open Compliance and Ethics Group's *Measurements and Metrics Guide (MMG)*, available at: *www.oceg.org/view/MMG*.)

For auditing and compliance efforts, performance measurement and reporting allows auditing and compliance professionals to work with their clients (and fellow employees) and other stakeholders to define the goals, the roadmap and the end state the organization is working toward. What ideal system of operation does the company want to have? What should be tested to see whether the company is achieving that goal? What should be improved? How can you measure performance to gauge how well that improvement is happening? Debating ahead of time what measures will be considered for the formal performance reporting will help ensure that everyone is on the same page and that surprises can be anticipated. In addition, we always say we need to improve communications (the number one cause of failure, by far, in most everything we do). Definition of your performance measurement and reporting program creates a vehicle for discussion on what's important, what your priorities are, and where you want to go. Knowing that makes an auditing project enormously easier. Performance measurement and reporting on organizational and auditing efforts offers a strategic opportunity for the compliance and the internal audit departments to influence the entire organization's governance efforts. Consider taking it on!

As mentioned, internal audit should weigh incorporating an evaluation of performance measurement and reporting into each audit performed. Auditing the organization-wide performance measurement and reporting program is also strongly recommended. An audit will provide for an independent and objective review of the efforts of the organization to define its goals and objectives, take action on them and monitor progress, including corrective actions as things happen (and they will happen). Evaluating the program involves defining the system to be audited; assessing the measures being used, the processes in place, and the operating effectiveness; and determining whether improvement to the system will have an effect on the organization's results.

Improving the organization's operational performance is always a critical priority, and implementing (or enhancing) a formal performance measurement and reporting program will help greatly. It ensures that the organization stays on track with its overall objectives; failing to audit that control creates a significant gap in the overall audit coverage.

CHAPTER 4: MY FAVORITES

The way to succeed is never quit. That's it. But really be humble about it.

Alex Haley

This chapter contains a series of excerpts from some of my favorite resources. I am sure you will find these references invaluable in your internal audit practice and research.

Auditing system conversions[1]

Internal auditors play a valuable role in ensuring that IT investments are well managed and have a positive impact on an organization. Their assurance role supports senior management, the audit committee, the Board of Directors and other stakeholders. Internal auditors need to take a risk-based approach in planning their many activities on IT project audits. With limited audit resources, auditors must focus on the highest-risk project areas, while adding value to the organization. Audit best practices suggest internal auditors should be involved throughout a project's life cycle – not just in post-implementation assessments.

---

[1] "Auditing System Conversions," *ITAudit*, Swanson D (March 2004), available at: *www.theiia.org/ITAuditArchive/index.cfm?act=ITAudit.archive&fid=5495*.

20 questions directors should ask about internal audit[2]

The questions in this briefing are designed to help directors understand the contribution of Internal Audit and to provide guidance to Audit Committee members on what to ask their Chief Audit Executives. With each question there is a brief discussion that provides background on the reasons for asking the question and, where appropriate, some recommended practices.

The role of auditing in public sector governance[3]

This practice guide presents information on the importance of the public sector audit activity to effective governance and defines the key elements needed to maximize the value the public sector audit activity provides to all levels of government. The practice guide is intended to point to the roles of audit (without differentiating between external and internal), methods by which those roles can be fulfilled, and the essential ingredients necessary to support an effective audit function.

Avoiding IS icebergs[4]

This article explores the audit's assurance role regarding information security and outlines approaches and methodologies.

---

[2] *20 Questions Directors Should Ask About Internal Audit*, Fraser J and Lindsay H, The Canadian Institute of Chartered Accountants (2004), available at: www.theiia.org/download.cfm?file=2927.
[3] *The Role of Auditing in Public Sector Governance*, The Institute of Internal Auditors (November 2006), available at: www.theiia.org/download.cfm?file=3512.
[4] "Avoiding IS Icebergs," *Information Security*, Swanson D (October 2000), available at: www.theiia.org/chapters/index.cfm/view.download/fileid/15002/cid/94.

Imagine you're the captain of the RMS Titanic, standing on the bridge as it steams across the frigid North Atlantic under a moonless sky. The ship's architect boasted of her invincibility, but you still station hands on the bow as lookouts for icebergs drifting in the black waters. After checking your course and issuing instructions to the crew, you retire for the evening, assured all is well. Several hours later, you're shocked out of your slumber by terrible vibrations and a horrific wail of buckling metal. Your worst fears are confirmed when you reach the bridge; the ship struck an iceberg despite your precautions. At this point, it doesn't matter how or why it happened; the damage is done and your ship is going to the bottom. What does this have to do with information security? The same scenario could happen to any organization that deploys security technologies and policies but doesn't audit its systems and personnel compliance. Routine, independent reviews of security systems and procedures not only ensure an organization has adequate protections in place, but confirm that they are working as designed and are effective.

OCEG *Internal Audit Guide* (OIAG)[5]

The OCEG *Internal Audit Guide* (OIAG) will help directors, executives and other senior managers charged with governance responsibilities to better understand the issues and processes involved in an internal audit of a compliance and ethics program. The IAG is designed primarily for the internal auditor, but it is also useful for compliance and ethics officers, compliance directors and board members. By applying the processes and practices

---

[5] *Internal Audit Guide*, OCEG (2006): *www.oceg.org/view/IAGExecSum*.

contained in the IAG, an organization will ensure that they have an effective compliance and ethics program in place.

The OCEG Internal Audit Guide (OIAG) can be used by:

- Internal auditors completing an internal audit of GRC capabilities.
- Audit committee members, to gain an understanding of the means to achieve GRC objectives.
- Oversight and strategic personnel, including those charged with governance responsibilities; those who need to understand the necessary and desirable components of a GRC capability, and how to implement appropriate mechanisms within their organization.
- GRC strategic and operational professionals, such as chief compliance and ethics officers, as the guide helps them to understand what to expect of an effective assessment program.
- Operational personnel who may be subject to GRC capability audit, as the guide provides useful preparatory information[6].

Overview

Organizations are exposed to governance, compliance and ethical risks daily. Coupled with the current economic, regulatory and social climate, these risks have propelled corporate governance, compliance management and integrity to a top business priority. More than ever, the business community perceives the need not only to articulate the principles of good governance, compliance,

---

[6] OCEG, available at: *www.oceg.org/view/IAG*.

risk management and ethics – but also to integrate these concepts into the fabric of day-to-day business – and use them to drive better performance. This need to put "principles into practice" sits at the very core of OCEG's efforts.

The availability of guidelines helps take much of the guesswork out of developing, managing and improving compliance and ethics programs. For investors, underwriters and other external stakeholders, these same guidelines provide a tool to help evaluate compliance efforts and to reward those organizations that excel.

The Open Compliance and Ethics Group (OCEG) is a not-for-profit organization with a clear public mission: to help organizations integrate and improve their governance, compliance and risk management activities to drive ethical business conduct and integrity (*www.oceg.org*). OCEG is committed to helping organizations reduce the financial and business risk associated with governance, compliance and ethical issues.

An effective internal audit (IA) function is a valuable resource for management, the Board and audit committee due to its understanding of the organization and its culture, operations and risk profile. The objectivity, skills and knowledge of competent internal auditors can contribute to the effectiveness of an organization's internal control, risk management and related governance processes. An internal audit of a compliance and ethics program can assist in improving the governance practices of an organization.

A governance "primer" from the OCEG *Internal Audit Guide* is provided in Appendix D.

4: My Favorites

Improving information technology (is always needed)[7]

Information Technology is everywhere – it is also a fundamental aspect of pretty well every single organizational process and a critical success factor for most, and maybe even all, business strategies. Organizations need to continually "invest" in improving their information technology practices and internal auditors can assist in that effort by providing objective and thoughtful improvement recommendations. Sponsors of the various organizational business initiatives play a particularly important role in successfully implementing change within the organization – (so) – rather than start from a blank page, or even with only a couple of long time favorites, I've consolidated 70 leading resources from a variety of sources.

IT audit, assurance, security and control standards[8]

ISACA Standards provide the information required to meet the compliance needs of Audit, Assurance and Control professionals, and also provide essential guidance to improve the effectiveness and efficiency of IT Audit and Assurance and IS Control Professionals. Knowledge of, and adherence to, ISACA Standards enables IT and IS professionals to approach their challenges with a risk-based approach that is in line with ISACA methodology.

---

[7] *Improving Information Technology (is always needed)*, AuditNet, Swanson D, available at: *www.auditnet.org/articles/DSIA201005.htm*.

[8] *IT Standards, Guidelines, and Tools and Techniques for Audit and Assurance and Control Professionals*, ISACA (March 2010), available at: *www.isaca.org/standards*.

Improving information security! (An endless task)[9]

Information security is a complicated subject – end of story. There are numerous stakeholders, an endless number of parties involved, and of course, that ever-changing risk landscape that too many times moves totally acceptable long-term practices to – we need that fixed by the end of the week! (What were you thinking?)

Information security involves technology and process, but it also involves people (and that's the rub). A culture of security takes time. For security to be truly effective large parts of the organization must be engaged and understand the scope of the challenges (and practices needed to address them). Always remember, the organization's reputation can be dramatically impacted with just a single front-page story. I've consolidated a comprehensive series of diverse resources (121 resources!) that includes concise articles, comprehensive papers and guides, and finally massive websites with an endless source of further guidance.

> The National Association of Corporate Directors, representing directors in the United States, has published guidance for board oversight of information security (*see the publications listed at www.nacdonline.org*). The NACD's reports give practical steps the Board can take to oversee IT security, such as learning the names of the people in charge, making sure they are qualified and ensuring that they have adequate resources. Such common sense solutions can go a long way in helping boards make a positive contribution to IT security.

---

[9] *Improving Information Security! (an endless task)*, AuditNet, Swanson D, available at: www.auditnet.org/articles/DSIA201006.htm.

Auditing compliance and ethics[10]

Broadly understood, compliance with an organization's policies and procedures is an important activity that helps make organizational governance effective. Monitoring and maintaining compliance is not just to keep the regulators happy; compliance with regulatory requirements and the organization's policies and procedures is a critical component of an effective enterprise-wide risk management program. It can also be one of the most important ways in which an organization achieves its business goals, sustains its ethical health, works towards long-term prosperity, and preserves and promotes its values.

This article provides an overview of a typical compliance and ethics program and discusses the challenges and processes involved in auditing an organization's compliance and ethics efforts.

---

[10] *Auditing Compliance and Ethics*, ACCA, Swanson D, available at: *www.accaglobal.com/members/publications/accounting_business/CPD/2898556*.

CHAPTER 5: IIA RELATED GUIDANCE

Man's mind, once stretched by a new idea, never regains its original dimension.

Oliver Holmes

I've had the privilege to participate in a variety of IIA papers over the years, presented below are excerpts from some of the more significant reports and internal audit guidance.

International Professional Practices Framework (IPPF)[11]

The IIA's *International Professional Practices Framework (IPPF)* is the authoritative guidance on the internal audit profession. The IPPF presents internationally consistent mandatory and strongly recommended guidance for the practice of internal auditing anywhere in the world.

About the internal audit profession[12]

Internal auditing is one of the cornerstones of corporate governance, along with the Board of Directors, senior management and external auditing. Because of an internal auditor's unique position within the organization, they provide audit committee members with valuable assistance by giving objective assurance on governance, risk

---

[11] *www.theiia.org/guidance/standards-and-guidance/interactive-ippf/.*
[12] *www.theiia.org/theiia/about-the-profession/about-the-internal-audit-profession/.*

management and control processes. To do this effectively, an internal audit activity must be adequately resourced, professionally staffed and follow the internationally recognized framework for internal auditing. Provided by The Institute of Internal Auditors (IIA), the *International Professional Practices Framework (IPPF)* comprises the *International Standards for the Professional Practice of Internal Auditing (Standards)*, Code of Ethics and Practice Advisories.

20 questions directors should ask about internal audit[13]

The questions in this briefing are designed to help directors understand the contribution of Internal Audit and to provide guidance to Audit Committee members on what to ask their Chief Audit Executives. With each question there is a brief discussion that provides background on the reasons for asking the question and, where appropriate, some recommended practices.

Organizational governance: guidance for internal auditors[14]

The topic of organizational governance (often referred to as *corporate governance*) is important for many key stakeholders in the political and business worlds. Typically, internal auditors operate in two capacities in this area. First, auditors provide independent, objective assessments on the

---

[13] *20 Questions Directors Should Ask About Internal Audit*, Fraser J and Lindsay H, The Canadian Institute of Chartered Accountants (2004), available at: *www.theiia.org/download.cfm?file=2927*.

[14] *Organizational Governance: Guidance for Internal Auditors*, The Institute of Internal Auditors (July 2006).

appropriateness of the organization's governance structure and the operating effectiveness of specific governance activities. Second, they act as catalysts for change, advising or advocating improvements to enhance the organization's governance structure and practices.

By providing assurance on the risk management, control, and governance processes within an organization, internal auditing is one of the key cornerstones of effective organizational governance. This guidance is designed to help internal auditing in its assurance and advisory role with regard to specific aspects of organizational governance.

The role of internal auditing in enterprise-wide risk management[15]

Risk management is a fundamental element of corporate governance. Management is responsible for establishing and operating the risk management framework on behalf of the Board. Enterprise-wide risk management brings many benefits as a result of its structured, consistent and coordinated approach. Internal auditor's core role in relation to ERM should be to provide assurance to management and to the Board on the effectiveness of risk management. When internal auditing extends its activities beyond this core role, it should apply certain safeguards, including treating the engagements as consulting services and, therefore, applying all relevant Standards. In this way, internal auditing will protect its independence and the

---

[15] *The Role of Internal Auditing in Enterprise-wide Risk Management*, The Institute of Internal Auditors (January 2009), available at: www.theiia.org/download.cfm?file=62465.

objectivity of its assurance services. Within these constraints, ERM can help raise the profile and increase the effectiveness of internal auditing.

The role of auditing in public sector governance[16]

This practice guide presents information on the importance of the public sector audit activity to effective governance and defines the key elements needed to maximize the value the public sector audit activity provides to all levels of government. The practice guide is intended to point to the roles of audit (without differentiating between external and internal), methods by which those roles can be fulfilled, and the essential ingredients necessary to support an effective audit function. As such, it may not be fully applicable in every jurisdiction, particularly where government audit roles and responsibilities are specifically defined to exclude certain functions or assign them to other entities.

Establishing an internal audit shop

"Have you ever been asked to set up a new internal audit shop?" The suggestions and resources available at this IIA informational repository can help you get started: *www.theiia.org/guidance/additional-resources/establishing-an-audit-shop/*.

---

[16] *The Role of Auditing in Public Sector Governance*, The Institute of Internal Auditors (November 2006), available at: *www.theiia.org/download.cfm?file=3512*.

5: IIA Related Guidance

The role of internal auditing in resourcing the internal audit activity[17]

When considering the resourcing of the internal audit activity a question that often arises is, "Who or what resources can be utilized to provide internal auditing?" In practice, organizations utilize a number of different alternatives ranging from a fully resourced activity housed within the organization to external resources obtained from outside the organization, or any combination thereof. This diversity of practice raises a question in some organizations concerning the optimum balance of internally and externally supplied resources. The purpose of this paper is to provide guidance and clarify the roles of the Board, management, and the chief audit executive on resourcing the internal audit activity and the various issues involved.

Internal control over financial reporting: guidance for smaller public companies[18]

This small business guidance takes the concepts of the 1992 *Internal Control - Integrated Framework* and demonstrates their applicability for achieving financial reporting objectives of smaller publicly traded companies.

---

[17] *The Role of Internal Auditing in Resourcing the Internal Audit Activity*, The Institute of Internal Auditors (January 2009), available at: *www.theiia.org/download.cfm?file=66876*.
[18] *Internal Control over Financial Reporting: Guidance for Smaller Public Companies, Volume 1: Executive Summary*, COSO (June 2006), available at: *www.theiia.org/download.cfm?file=53359*.

COSO Enterprise Risk Management: Integrated Framework[19]

The underlying premise of enterprise risk management is that every entity exists to provide value for its stakeholders. All entities face uncertainty, and the challenge for management is to determine how much uncertainty to accept as it strives to grow stakeholder value.

Uncertainty presents both risk and opportunity, with the potential to erode or enhance value. Enterprise risk management enables management to effectively deal with uncertainty and associated risk and opportunity, enhancing the capacity to build value. Value is maximized when management sets strategy and objectives to strike an optimal balance between growth and return goals and related risks, and efficiently and effectively deploys resources in pursuit of the entity's objectives.

---

[19] *Enterprise Risk Management: Integrated Framework, Executive Summary*, COSO (September 2004), available at: *www.theiia.org/download.cfm?file=9229*.

CHAPTER 6: PRIORITIES FOR THE COMING DECADE

The most important contribution management needs to make in the 21st century is to increase the productivity of knowledge work and the knowledge worker.

Peter F. Drucker

Auditing your enterprise risk management program

Everyone talks about the need for good risk management programs, but nobody seems to know how to audit them to ensure they actually work. Who bears responsibility for setting the parameters of an enterprise risk management (ERM) program is pretty clear: the Board of Directors and the C-level executives. They decide what the risks are, what level of risk they're willing to tolerate, and what risks they do not want to tolerate. They are responsible for monitoring and responding to ERM outputs and obtaining assurance that the organization's risks are acceptably managed within the boundaries specified. Also, remember that risk management is not an end in itself; it has value only if it assists a company to achieve its business objectives over the long term. Internal auditors, in both their assurance and consulting roles, contribute to ERM in a variety of ways. They spend most of their time assessing how effectively management has responded to key risks by developing adequate operations and control structures. Fundamentally, the audit team provides the Board and management with an objective assessment of the company's ERM efforts, including where the company can improve.

Why care whether ERM works?

According to the Committee of Sponsoring Organizations, ERM is:

... a process, effected by an entity's board of directors, management, and other personnel, applied in strategy setting and across the enterprise, designed to identify potential events that may affect the entity, manage risk to be within its risk appetite, and to provide reasonable assurance regarding the achievement of entity objectives.

Notice the process view – that is, risk management is more than a risk management system. Alternatively, as a friend of mine puts it, ERM is how you address uncertainty around organizational goals.

From an internal audit perspective, inadequate identification of key risks to an organization increases the likelihood of bad events occurring. Improper identification can result in wasting resources on areas of low risk with little reward. Conversely, it can leave a company more exposed to negative events. (An example from the financial industry: At banks and mortgage companies, how much of a priority did the Boards place on oversight of lending activities? Not much, I'd say, and look where it got them.)

Still, even if top management effectively identifies its key risks, the company still needs assurance that its response to those risks is effective. An effective response is a crucial part of ERM, and that means attention to the design and operation of internal controls. Indeed, an *informal* response to key risks *increases* vulnerability to something going awry. Strong controls must exist and work for ERM to be effective, so, enter the internal auditor.

Risk is perfectly fine at an acceptable level, but management must define what that acceptable level is in the interest of achieving the company's goals. Using another banking example, management might challenge the Board to define the point at which losses from bad loans become unacceptable. If a $1 million loan goes bad, will the Board become concerned? What about a $10 million loan? The specific number tends to change over time, so the question must be asked periodically to maintain an understanding of the correct risk appetite. Furthermore, banks face many other potential causes of loss as well, and some of them cannot be expressed in pure monetary terms. (Think of the cost of adverse publicity after a customer data theft.)

An audit of ERM should determine whether significant risks to the organization are appropriately identified and assessed on an ongoing basis. It should also confirm that those risks are monitored for possible changes, that risk management techniques (insurance, hedging, and the like) are in place, and that management has the ability to recognize and respond to new risks as they arise.

The guts of an ERM audit

An audit can focus solely on the effectiveness of the ERM program if you want, but it can also be extended to look at ERM *efficiency*. Auditors can provide assurance that information about risks and the management of them is collected, summarized and reported properly to the appropriate level of the governance structure.

There are two distinct elements to most ERM audits: evaluating the design and implementation of the program as a management system, and evaluating the operational practices of the program, including an assessment of the risks currently being managed.

In general, internal auditors should assure management and the Board that everything that should be done to manage risks is being done. Auditors should also provide guidance on control effectiveness and feedback on managerial decisions and results. Further issues worth considering in an ERM audit include:

- Are the organization's risk management efforts appropriate to its needs? This includes management's recognition of, and response to, emerging obligations and opportunities in risk management and corporate governance.
- Has an effective risk management program been developed and implemented? Is accountability well established and acknowledged by those to be held accountable? Has management and audit agreed on the program's definition?
- Are there appropriate systems, policies, procedures and guidelines relating to ERM, supported by suitable awareness, training and compliance activities?
- Has the organization embraced the risk management philosophy? Is executive management seen as a strong proponent, and is the consideration of risk an integral part of day-to-day business decisions?
- How successful are the risk management efforts? This is a tricky question to answer given the inherent uncertainties in risk, but a retrospective review of the organization's identification of and response to risks, including incidents that indicate inadequate controls, should be revealing.
- Do we need to increase the understanding of our key risks and what else needs to be done? Have we done everything necessary to get a grip on enterprise-level risks?

6: Priorities for the Coming Decade

Internal audit's role in risk management

The Institute of Internal Auditors proposes that risk management activities be divided into three groups. One includes internal auditors providing assurances, as discussed above. A second group includes activities exclusively related to management decisions, such as selecting risk appetite and risk responses. (This second group of risk management activities should not be done by internal audit as they are deemed to be management activities.) The third group includes risk management activities that may be performed by internal audit when there are safeguards in place. Safeguards may be things like changing the internal audit charter to include these added responsibilities and receiving acknowledgements from management regarding their responsibilities.

Fundamentally, enterprise risk management is not a new concept. What perhaps is new is the importance of bringing risk management into the management decision-making process and ensuring a corporate view of the relationships between risks in different parts of the organization is regularly evaluated and responded to.

Risk management is inherent in every organization. Any manager or employee who has been given objectives will almost unconsciously assess the things that will prevent them from reaching their goal. At a minimum they will manage those risks in an informal *ad hoc* way. ERM is a high-level formalization of this natural process. As a formal process, it needs a coordinator to draw from all areas of the organization key risks and current efforts to mitigate them. We also need to move from a focus on risk identification to a focus on how best to manage our significant risks. Finally, the goal of risk management is not to reduce uncertainty. It is, rather, to help organizations make better decisions and to respond more intelligently when the unexpected inevitably occurs.

> **The bottom line**: risk management needs to be integrated into the organization's entire operations from board oversight to senior management's strategic planning and leadership, to the operating management's day-to-day operational control. Perhaps this is nothing new, but certainly it is important to the organization's long-term success and worthy of a formal evaluation by internal audit.

Internal audit's seat at the governance table

In June 1999, the Institute of Internal Auditors approved a new definition for internal auditing. Internal auditing was described as "an independent, objective assurance and consulting activity," which isn't exactly news. Instead, the telling phrase came at the end of the revised IIA definition – which said internal auditing should be brought to bear on a company's risk management, internal control and governance processes. For many years, the IIA has advocated that internal audit should be one of the cornerstones of good governance. The IIA has issued a global position statement regarding organizational governance that discusses the many roles that internal auditing can play in an organization's governance effort; a few are discussed in this article.

You can audit governance?

Governance activities exist to help a company meet its objectives in being well run and accountable to its stakeholders. Just like in any other activity, management and the Board will want to articulate their objectives in each area and put programs in place to achieve those objectives. An often-used definition of organizational governance comes from the Paris-based forum of democratic markets, the Organization for Economic Co-operation and Development (OECD):

Corporate governance involves a set of relationships between a company's management, its board, its shareholders, and other stakeholders. Corporate governance also provides the structure through which the objectives of the company are set, and the means of attaining those objectives and monitoring performance are determined.

Components of governance that internal audit can provide assurance or consulting services include:

- board structure, objectives and dynamics
- board committee functions
- the Board policy manual
- processes for maintaining awareness of governance requirements
- board education and training
- proper assignment of accountabilities and performance management
- completeness of ethics policies and codes of conduct
- communication and acceptance of ethics policies and codes of conduct
- management evaluation and compensation
- recruitment processes for senior management and board members
- employee training
- governance self-assessments
- comparison with governance codes or best practices

- external communications.

What internal audit brings to the table

Typically, internal auditors operate in two capacities regarding governance. First, auditors provide independent, objective assessments on the appropriateness of the company's governance structure and the operating effectiveness of specific governance activities. Second, they act as catalysts for change, advising or advocating improvements to enhance the organization's governance structure and practices. By providing assurance on the risk management, control and governance processes within an organization, internal auditing is one of the cornerstones of effective organizational governance. In auditing the risk management processes used by the organization, internal audit might recommend that a more formal enterprise-wide, risk management program be considered by the Board and management. In consulting with the CEO or CFO, internal audit could recommend that the terms of reference for key organizational oversight committees (management's and the Board's) be updated – and most likely expanded – to tackle the many emerging governance requirements facing most organizations today.

How to earn that seat at the table

Auditing the financial transactions that have been processed within accounting is straightforward: review for proper authorization, assess supporting evidence for appropriateness of transactions, test for accuracy and completeness of financial reporting and then communicate your findings to management. By comparison, auditing governance can be complex and somewhat subjective. For example, try evaluating whether a proper "tone at the top" exists in the organization, or whether the Board and management reinforce the code of conduct properly – and follow it themselves!

Defining the scope of governance processes is a first step. What are we looking at, and who is responsible for what? Obtaining a consensus on what the performance measures are can be another challenging planning activity. Remember, in auditing governance you want to ensure the areas selected for review are ones that have the largest potential for improvement, or are in highest need of confirmation that they are operating effectively. Obtaining the support of your audit committee chairman and your CEO is absolutely critical.

Having the skills and experience required to perform the audit task is also a must. The role internal audit plays in governance is highly influenced by the maturity level of the organization's governance processes and structure and the role and qualification of internal auditors. When there is much to do in formalizing and strengthening governance efforts, internal audit will likely focus more on providing advice regarding the best structure and good practices to consider. Where governance is very structured and operating relatively effectively, the audit would likely focus on identifying further improvement opportunities and assessing the performance of key controls and practices. Benchmarking the company's governance practices to similar organizations could be very beneficial. Assessing compliance with published and respected governance codes could offer another quick win for internal audit and the organization.

Bringing transparency to governance

Ask for a report card from internal audit; identifying improvement opportunities is the first step in continuous improvement. Consider inviting your chief audit executive to provide an opinion on the organization's governance practices; it certainly will provide a learning opportunity for all stakeholders involved in your organization, and obtaining an independent and objective assessment of this key activity (governing the organization) might just be what's needed to take your governance practices to the next level of transparency.

Are you protecting your digital assets?

Safeguarding assets has been an important objective of all organizations for centuries. In today's digital age, however, what does safeguarding your assets really mean? Who is responsible for it? How is "protection" actually achieved? The COSO framework for enterprise risk management recognized the importance of safeguarding assets as an implicit component of effective internal control. Its landmark 1992 framework even defined internal control as:

[A] process ... designed to provide reasonable assurance regarding the achievement of objectives in the following categories: effectiveness and efficiency of operations; reliability of financial reporting; and compliance with applicable laws and regulations.

You can't provide reasonable assurance of your operations or financial reporting unless you know what your assets are, where they are, and who is doing what with them. You need to know your assets are protected. Before 2000, protecting an organization's assets consisted mainly of physical safeguards, asset management (for example, taking inventory of your goods), and monitoring asset values. Although these practices are still critical in today's business environment, additional processes, procedures and controls are required to protect our information assets. With a high percentage of market value now accounted for by intangible assets such as intellectual property, reputation, brand and electronic records, information is now a vital business resource. As with physical assets in earlier post-industrial times, the vulnerability of today's valuable informational assets to theft or other criminal attack has made protection of such assets a matter of immense urgency for all organizations.

Who is responsible for information asset protection?

While chief information security officers and chief financial officers are important players regarding information asset protection and security, they are not the true "guardians" of the organization's critical informational assets. For example, in hospitals, CFOs are not responsible for safeguarding patient records; at insurance companies, they are not the guardians of policyholder records. In the pharmaceutical or technology sectors, the company's crown jewels (its intellectual property) are not the direct responsibility of the CFO or the CISO (chief information security officer).

All of these forms of data have associated expenses and are used to generate revenues (billings, annual fees, royalties), for which the CISO has ultimate security oversight. The CISO, in turn, must ensure the integrity of the chain of custody by enforcing rules applicable to key managers and other authorized personnel in their roles as the day-to-day "guardians." In short, internal control is affected by people at every level of an organization. In fact, many managers are more directly responsible for day-to-day asset protection than the CISO or CFO.

What are the implications?

Addressing the following questions will help determine key implications of how to protect digital assets and what actions to take.

- Will an organization's information-security management system become critical to the safeguarding of the CFO's financial records? Will those systems emerge as the key means of safeguarding an organization's assets?
- Will CFOs and finance staff need to understand and implement informational asset protection measures to be effective in their roles of supporting the guardians of the organization's assets?
- Will more guidance be needed on the definition, classification and protection of information assets?
- Will CISOs need to work more closely with and educate the finance function (and all operating departments, really) about how to best implement a sustainable information protection and security program?
- Should the organization establish a data management function and data governance policy, standards and procedures? Both the function and governance could be headed by a senior manager reporting to the chief operating officer or chief executive officer. What role(s) could the chief information officer (CIO) take in information protection?
- Will the Board and CEO need to provide more in the way of expectations?

- Will internal audit and external audit spend more resources on evaluating the protection of all of an organization's assets, physical and digital?

The internal audit function in particular needs to think more strategically about enterprise-wide security and ensure that enterprise-wide risk management is a guiding theme for prioritizing the organization's efforts.

The big question: what should we do?

First, top management must convene a council of chief-level executives including the CEO, CFO, CIO, CISO, CAE (chief audit executive) and other chiefs, including compliance, risk management and all areas of the business that own, maintain, use, or rely upon information. The most senior members of this council must ensure all members understand the critical reliance on information security and the financial, regulatory, social and other impacts that can befall the organization, if information security is breached. This understanding must be expressed in non-technical business terms to ensure everyone competently understands the level(s) of risk the organization can and cannot accept with regard to protecting information assets. Only with this comprehensive level of understanding can management ensure resources dedicated to information security are in line with the criticality of protection required by the organization.

As a next step, this C-level council must collectively ensure the security resources and solutions in place are appropriate to manage the business risks within the bounds of external requirements and the business appetite for risks. Security monitoring must ensure the appropriate level of protection will remain in place and functioning.

The bottom-line

Top management must implement an information-security management program that truly safeguards all assets of the organization. Organizations that have not done so already should immediately:

- discuss information security with the Board and senior management, ensuring their understanding of the key risks and gaining their support for the necessary controls
- link security investments and resourcing to core business priorities and risk assessment results
- leverage existing security standards, guidance and practices and define the organization's information security management system
- explicitly assign responsibility and accountability for protecting informational assets across the organization
- revisit IT and related strategies to align business and IT efforts, and ensure that overarching information security requirements are explicitly defined
- inventory and classify the organization's information: identify it, assign a business guardian to it, and determine how best to protect it based on risk assessment results
- implement common security practices and solutions to meet business needs and comply with ever expanding regulatory compliance requirements
- identify continuous improvement opportunities and prioritize them, and then invest in improving the operational resilience of the organization

- strengthen the business continuity program
- configure security into both business processes and the supporting IT systems, to strengthen technical and procedural security practices
- include "asset protection in the digital age" as one of the discussion items in quarterly business performance review meetings, and develop action plans for improvement as needed.

We must build security *into* and *across* all organizational efforts. The CISO and CFO each have a mandate to work with the other key corporate players – and especially the business guardians of informational assets – to ensure effective asset protection. This is definitely a responsibility shared by various players throughout the organization. The question is, do the players work together to ensure effective asset protection? Or do they work on this critical responsibility in silos, allowing things to fall between the cracks? Are we also addressing information protection in all the outsourced activities that are so prevalent today?

Leaders also need to ensure that all vendors, suppliers and other third parties responsible for protecting information used in outsourced activities are included in the mix of information asset protection and security actions.

As a colleague recently indicated, we need to move away from financial, operational and technological thinking and decisions toward a critical-thinking methodology meant to maximize the benefit to the enterprise as a whole, not sub-units of it. That is, based on enterprise-wide risk assessment and management.

Are all your organization's assets appropriately protected in the digital age? I recommend making this a topic of discussion at your next management committee meeting, or better yet, put it on the Board agenda. An effective tone at the top starts with top management and the Board taking action to implement appropriate security controls.

Operational resiliency: a business priority!

As I've mentioned before, ensuring that an organization can recover from disaster is a basic business requirement the Board should explore regularly with management. Nowadays, leading companies are taking this requirement and turning it into a strategic advantage: namely, investments in operational resiliency are assisting organizations to become more responsive to client needs, as well as improving operational reliability, quality and efficiency. It is an effort you should embrace, too. Operational resiliency covers a huge waterfront, and a universally agreed-upon definition of it continues to be elusive. To some, its focus is purely on IT recovery capabilities, where investments in network and software redundancy are the priority. For others (usually business managers), it means strengthening the business unit's recovery capabilities, which brings a focus to business continuity plans. For still others (senior executives and board members), it is the organization's ability to respond to emergencies and meet client needs. I believe operational resiliency covers all of the above.

As companies face increasingly complex business and operational environments, functions such as security and business continuity keep evolving; indeed, they *need* to keep evolving. Today, successful security and business continuity programs (BCP) both address the technical issues involved *and* strive to support the organization's efforts to improve and sustain an adequate level of operational resiliency. Operational resiliency efforts tackle operational risk by identifying potential operational problems and improving the processes and systems used; that is, how operational problems are reduced over the longer term.

Being able to continue critical business functions while responding to a major disaster, and then to return to normal operations efficiently and cohesively afterwards, is a critical success factor for all organizations. Effective business continuity and disaster recovery (DR) programs are vital and have become a necessary cost of doing business. They must receive adequate management attention and support, if the company is to survive and remain competitive in a post-disaster situation. The purpose of the BCP and DR programs is to prepare the organization to cope more effectively with major disruption. Business managers plan possible responses in advance of the actual incident (or incidents), rather than simply responding in the heat of the moment. This planning increases the quality and *consistency* of the response – that is, it makes the operation resilient to disruption – regardless of the person who executes the plan.

Taking this effort to the next level, management needs to enhance its operational culture, processes and systems, by strengthening the reliability and efficiency of each. An organization's operational resiliency program should be an umbrella effort; that is, it should provide support and guidance for the organization's information security, BCP, DR and emergency management program efforts. The following questions should be considered as part of any effort to improve operational resiliency:

- Are security and business continuity activities planned in a coordinated manner in your organization, or are they performed in silos? Are they viewed as technical, rather than business, activities?
- Can you actively manage operational resiliency, or do you typically react to disruptive events as they occur?
- Do you know if the security and business continuity practices you've implemented are effective? Have you tested them? Do they support the achievement of the organization's strategic objectives and mission?
- Can you measure the success of your security and business continuity activities? Can you consistently repeat and sustain that success over the long run? Have you benchmarked your activities against others in your industry, or against independent third-party guidelines?
- Do you have a foundation from which to continuously improve your security and business continuity efforts?

Internal auditing's contribution

Internal audits of information security, BCP and DR programs are highly recommended. The Board and management need assurance regarding the effectiveness of those efforts, and they also need assurance that the company is building a more efficient and effective operation. During every internal audit project, auditors should consider including an evaluation of the business unit's efforts to be more efficient and effective, and in particular, consider what initiatives are being implemented to enhance operational resiliency. Over time, internal audit's focus on assessing management's efforts to make operations more reliable will support the company's efforts to improve enterprise-wide processes and systems.

The following aspects are generally worth considering when scoping an audit of operational resiliency efforts:

- **Overall program governance.** How is operational resiliency being encouraged? Is the program given appropriate strategic direction and investment? (That is, does the organization place sufficient emphasis on operational improvement?) Are suitable sponsors and stakeholders involved, representing all critical parts of the organization? Do they take sufficient interest in the program, demonstrating their support through involvement and action? Most importantly of all, who is accountable for the program's success or failure?
- **Ongoing program management.** A critical success factor in every BCP and DR effort is the way in which the programs are planned and driven, ensuring that they meet objectives despite the company's inevitable competing priorities. Does program management balance consideration of the many conflicting priorities managers face with the critical need that corporate resiliency efforts be appropriate? This is not a once-a-year exercise anymore; being prepared is an ongoing, day-in and day-out effort.
- **Management of system or process changes.** The evaluation of operational resiliency inevitably results in system and process improvement. Is change management handled effectively to provide the best assurance that improvement results are beneficial and that operational reliability is occurring?

A long-term investment

Companies that want to implement a culture of continuous improvement should focus on improving the operational resiliency of key systems and processes. Internal audit should reinforce this goal by evaluating both the whole enterprise's and the individual business units' efforts to address operational risk by enhancing operational processes and systems. Building the resilient organization takes a long-term view and a persistent investment of management's time and resources, and leading organizations are doing this. Finally, being aware of what is important to your customers is critical to your success.

PART 2: IT AUDITING

CHAPTER 7: TACKLING IT AUDIT

The beginning of knowledge is the discovery of something we do not understand.

Frank Herbert

The importance of auditing IT projects well

Change to a company's IT infrastructure is a significant source of risk for every business. To protect the corporate crown jewels, robust change-management practices are absolutely critical. The need for a positive "control environment" within IT and a very unforgiving attitude regarding unauthorized IT changes cannot be overstated. In fact, a recent study by the IT Process Institute indicates that "best of breed" IT shops outperform their counterparts by a huge margin on many different performance indices. The two controls that were almost universally present in these high performers were:

- monitoring systems for unauthorized changes
- having defined consequences for intentional, unauthorized changes.

Internal audit's role regarding the implementation of IT initiatives varies widely, but also provides a significant opportunity for internal audit to deliver real value to the Board and executive management. That is, internal auditors should play an important role in ensuring that IT investments are well managed and have a positive effect on an organization. A well-managed IT project is absolutely critical to this success. IT efforts are getting more complicated each year; operational changes are becoming more challenging with each new technology being adopted, particularly where global operations are now being supported. The system integration requirements continue to amaze even the most experienced IT and audit professional.

An audit of an IT initiative can take many forms. At its simplest, the auditor can review the business case and hold a few interviews with key stakeholders. At its most complex, a full-time audit team will participate in almost every aspect of the IT project. This diversity depends on the risks involved and the assurance requirements of the Board and executive management. If the organization would totally unravel if the IT initiative fails, a "health check up" by internal audit can be very worthwhile.

Auditing major IT initiatives

The Board and management want to know many things regarding their IT efforts: that the IT efforts are productive; that the IT investments will have an impact; that their system of internal control is enhanced and strengthened by their IT efforts; and that the next disaster (from a failed IT implementation) will not happen. An independent assessment of an IT initiative can provide that feedback and prevent trouble down the road, or perhaps even prevent a business failure. Defining the audit goals, objectives and scope for a review of an IT initiative is a key first step. The internal auditor's involvement with an IT initiative typically involves reviewing and assessing the overall project plan and project management.

Auditors also need to assess the accuracy and completeness of the systems and data requirements for the proposed IT solution, by:

- evaluating and monitoring management's project plans for the various system changes that will be required
- assessing the completeness and appropriateness of management's systems and database design, including security and privacy aspects
- reviewing the user-acceptance and parallel-test planning and results to demonstrate successful end-to-end system operations and the "preparedness" for implementation (in a parallel test, the project team simultaneously tests both the old and new systems using the same data and compares their results in a comprehensive manner)
- reviewing the start-up of production systems and associated client data to ensure data integrity is maintained and "back out" plans in the event of a problem will be effective.

In addition, auditors need to assess the accuracy and completeness of the start-up of operational responsibilities within the organization (for the new IT "solution") by:

- evaluating and monitoring management's project plans for the various operational requirements
- assessing the completeness and appropriateness of the operational policies and procedures that are developed, and the related training.

The organization's various IT initiatives cover a broad span of technologies and, just as importantly, they affect business operations in a variety of ways. The planning phase of the audit needs to ensure the proper focus of the audit efforts. Internal auditors need to determine the level of their involvement and the best audit approach to take (during the IT initiative's initiation phase). The audit involvement decision should be based on the audit-risk assessment, and include factors such as the team's project-management experience, level of management involvement, size and complexity of the initiative, and effect on the organization if the initiative is delayed or unsuccessfully implemented. The most appropriate audit approach also needs to be defined during the audit project-planning phase.

Key issues to explore during the audit include:

- effective project sponsorship and project management (two absolutely critical factors in every IT project)
- accuracy of the business requirements
- representation of all stakeholder groups on the team
- existence of a robust IT risk management process.

Encouraging better performance

Like most audits, the audit of an IT initiative generally will involve three phases: planning, fieldwork and audit reporting. IT initiatives, however, come in many shapes and sizes, so the audit of an IT initiative must be flexible and risk based.

During the planning phase, the internal audit team should ensure that all key issues are considered, that the audit objectives will meet the organization's assurance needs, and that everyone involved understands the IT initiative that is being audited. It is important that the audit focuses on evaluating the significant components of the IT initiative – to use a risk-based approach to find the project elements most likely to fail or most in need of confirmation. The planning phase also should confirm that the audit scope is appropriate.

In the fieldwork phase, the auditor analyzes the IT initiative's various components based on the goals and methodology identified in the planning phase. Among some of the most important questions to answer are:

- Have the business requirements been clearly defined?
- Will the IT solution meet those requirements?
- Has the IT solution been proven to work?
- Is the IT solution secure and will privacy of information be maintained?
- Has the amount of effort involved reflected the risk involved with the solution's implementation?

Audit tests could include: reviewing business-case documentation and system-related documents; interviewing key participants in the project; looking at training materials and development of procedures for the solution's operation; and reviewing test plans, their results and management's communications to employees regarding preparation for implementation.

The audit-reporting phase is where the internal auditor ensures that all stakeholders are informed of the audit results and management's plans to enhance the IT initiative's efforts. Audit reporting can be straightforward: tell them what you did, what you found and what management plans to do.

The difference with auditing an IT initiative is that audit feedback needs to begin as early as possible, so change in project plans and efforts can be considered. Therefore, formal, ongoing feedback should be provided to the management of the IT initiative and senior management, and even the audit committee, on occasion, should be briefed with periodic status reports. Formal end-of-audit reporting is still needed, but any "news" from the audit team must be conveyed long before the audit report is formally issued.

We need to encourage IT process improvement

Auditing best practices recommend that internal auditors should be involved throughout an IT initiative's life cycle, not just in post-implementation evaluations (where the wounded are shot). An internal audit of an IT initiative also needs to be part of a broader IT audit plan as one audit does not assess the IT function's overall performance. It is a long-term assessment of IT efforts where true IT process improvement can be encouraged. For example, does the organization have a robust IT risk management process? Is IT implementing comprehensive patch- and change-management practices? Has the development and implementation process been updated to reflect today's significant security and privacy requirements? Is there an overall organizational project office?

Auditors can bring considerable value to an organization by evaluating both the IT and organizational aspects of an IT initiative. Because a conversion to a new IT solution is one of the highest risks that an organization can face, internal auditors' involvement and independent assessment of the issues and project plans will provide value far in excess of the audit's costs.

Auditing a company's IT strategies

Today's IT solutions are complex, and they are getting more challenging to implement all the time. One of the great questions for management at any company these days is simply whether all the investment in those systems is worth it. Internal auditing can play a critical role there, measuring and inspecting how the IT investment process – specifically, the management of IT investment – works. There are two distinct elements to most IT investment audits. They are the evaluation of:

- how that management process is "scoped out," designed, and implemented
- how that management process then operates, including an assessment of the business priorities currently being addressed.

An audit of IT investment management should identify whether the various management processes involved are operating well and what the key opportunities for improvement would be. The audit should evaluate whether management has an effective investment prioritization process in place, including the ongoing identification of changes in business priorities and new business opportunities. IT investment management also involves the evaluation of performance of IT initiatives, and the audit should assess the performance monitoring completed by management.

In general, an audit of investment management should allow internal auditors to provide: an opinion on process effectiveness, an assessment of the organization's efforts to align IT with business priorities, and assurance to the Board and management that the organization is working on the right projects.

Ten questions to answer

Audits of any IT system, and especially audits of how IT investment is working, will have many questions. Exactly which ones you'll need to answer and include in your audit planning will depend on your company's specific circumstances, but I've listed 10 of the most important ones below.

Question 1: Are the organization's planning activities appropriate to its needs?

The planning process should support management's awareness of, and response to, new and emerging business opportunities. The scope and formality of planning needs to be in line with the organization's needs and complexity.

Question 2: Has an effective IT investment management process been developed and implemented?

Every company needs a process to decide which initiative gets funding. Every company should also consider a balanced investment in operational, tactical and strategic IT areas. Of course, the level of funding in each category will vary widely depending on the business environment a company faces and the strategic direction it is taking. However, all of those areas should at least be considered, even if the funds devoted to any specific one is zero.

Question 3: Is accountability well established and acknowledged by those to be held accountable?

Management and staff need to know what they are responsible for. When it comes to management of IT investment management, we want to ensure that IT investments support the company's business and business efforts. This requires an investment decision-making process that is clear and relatively transparent. Identify the people at your company who participate in that process, and make sure they understand the consequences when the decisions they make produce bad results.

Question 4: Are there appropriate systems, policies, procedures and guidelines relating to IT investment management?

Describing how things get done is always beneficial. For something as important as, "Are we working on the right projects?" formal policies and procedures are worthwhile.

Question 5: How successful is IT in meeting business needs?

Assessing whether your company is effective overall is always challenging. Perhaps the best we can achieve is determining what the key opportunities for improvement are.

Question 6: Do we need to increase the alignment of IT efforts and business efforts? If so, what else needs to be done?

At the end of the day, a company and its IT department must do everything necessary to get a grip on the organization's IT investment priorities to ensure the company is focused on business priorities – rather than on IT systems.

Question 7: Does management have a strategic IT plan that is updated regularly and supports the annual plans, budgets and priorities of the various IT projects?

Companies should define the long-term direction of their IT needs, and auditors should be able to see a rationalization of what the company's IT spending priorities are, and why. Ideally, an IT strategic plan would be developed and approved by the Board, although the documentation may take many forms, such as a separate IT plan combined with the organization's overall business plan, or a series of business case submissions over time. The auditor should look for a demonstration of an overall strategic planning process regarding IT investment and IT spending prioritization. Also, remember that business planning should drive the IT priorities and IT investment decisions, which means both corporate management and IT management will need to be interviewed.

Question 8: What level of investment in IT and IT security has occurred over the past two to three years, and what is planned for the next two to three years?

In other words, are IT expenditures reasonable compared to the overall operating and capital budgets? While no specific level of investment in IT is deemed to be appropriate, the auditor should assess the reasonableness of the IT and security expenditures in relation to the overall capital and operating budgets. They should also review whether the expenditure trend line can be explained by the business and IT plans. Is there a process in place to manage the expenditures involved with IT and IT security?

Question 9: Have performance indicators for the IT function and IT security been developed? Are those indicators periodically reported to the Board?

Auditors should know what major issues have been reported regarding IT and IT security. A healthy debate should exist at the Board level when these issues are presented by management (and yes, management should be presenting these issues to the Board).

Question 10: Does management monitor IT's performance, as well as its capability to continue providing the services upon which the organization relies?

This question explores the monitoring of IT operations that management performs – and whether it is outsourced or managed internally, monitoring should be done. The formality of the monitoring can vary greatly, although outsourced arrangements probably need more monitoring, and so it should happen more frequently.

> **The bottom line**: Management of IT investment must be integrated into the organization's ongoing strategic planning effort and ensure that IT efforts consistently contribute to the organization's priorities. Perhaps it is time executive management revisited how it defines IT investment priorities. An audit is a good place to start.

Ensuring technology changes are well managed

Information technology is critical to the long-term success of most organizations. It is a key reason for the cost of operations, and cost of operations tends to be a vital component of overall profitability. It facilitates the introduction of new business initiatives, as well as the ongoing improvement of current processes, and allows the management team to monitor and report on performance. IT enables business operations through connectivity, information processing, business intelligence, and the like. Lastly, and especially important to this audience, IT can contribute greatly to a company's system of internal control.

With the organizational importance of IT continuing to grow each year, the importance of "change management" in IT systems continues to grow along with it. There is a substantial body of evidence that change management contributes critically to the implementation of efficient, effective, and secure IT operations. Because every change in an IT system creates a potential consequence on the company's operations, executives must understand change management thoroughly: how to impose it, how to enforce it and how to monitor and improve its effectiveness.

Research from the IT Process Institute has shown that organizations that manage their technology well perform substantially better than organizations that don't.

Simply stated, all IT changes need to be authorized and tested, and unauthorized or untested changes prohibited. Put another way: changes to a company's IT infrastructure are a significant source of risk for every business; to protect the corporate crown jewels, robust change management practices are absolutely critical. The need for a positive "control environment" within IT and an unforgiving attitude regarding unauthorized IT changes cannot be overstated.

Strong change management means planned system implementations, proven (read: tested) solutions, scheduled upgrade windows where recovery is facilitated, if needed, and much more. To manage technology changes well, a change management program needs to be formally introduced into the organization. Implementing a change management program means assigning responsibility for the various change activities involved in implementing new technology solutions.

Auditing technology change processes

An audit of change management should review IT results to identify key improvement opportunities. During the audit of change management programs, auditors need to:

- understand the change management processes and procedures
- identify and assess key controls within the change management processes that ensure all changes are properly authorized and tested prior to implementation
- determine the quality of the information generated by the change management program, and assess whether it is sufficient to manage the change management process
- assess change management performance metrics for their existence, effectiveness, monitoring activities, and responses to any program deviations
- evaluate whether risk management controls are preventive, detective, or corrective, and if a good balance has been implemented
- define tests to confirm the operational effectiveness of change management activities, including management and staff interviews, documentation and report reviews, and data analyses
- recommend opportunities for improvement of change management activities.

Indicators of poor change management

- **Unauthorized changes**: Anything above zero is unacceptable. Establishing a tone at the top that clearly communicates the company's intolerance of unauthorized changes is fundamental to the long-term success of change management programs.
- **Unplanned outages**: System outages should be scheduled (planned) to reduce the impact on the organization's operations. Predetermined "change windows" are where production systems should be updated. Unplanned outages are caused by system

problems and encourage a reactionary environment (that is, fire-fighting), which is not how you stay on top of internal control systems.

- **Low change success rate**: Good change management involves good testing; if changes have to be "backed out," it is an indicator of poor testing that failed to catch problems in the early stages.
- **High number of emergency changes**: Again, emergencies should be emergencies, and happen infrequently. Poor planning of changes result in a high number of emergencies.
- **Delayed project implementations**: Delays in project implementation are a sign of unrealistic plans or poor resourcing decisions. Good change management practices encourage good planning and, over time, more achievable plans, resulting in fewer delays and cancellation of implementations.

An audit of change management should review the above risk indicators as a good measure of the likelihood that controls are or are not effective. Auditing IT processes can be very productive; good business results happen due to the quality of the processes used to produce them. Reviewing the policies and procedures and related processes that have been implemented will help determine whether your IT investments will be productive and worthwhile. Also, discussing with IT management how they do their jobs – in particular their IT change efforts – will be extremely productive, and help answer the fundamental question: Are changes being implemented in a controlled or haphazard manner?

When I look at the work IT managers have done to test (that is, prove) that a change is working, I want to see four fundamental testing techniques: functional testing, stress testing, logical testing and path testing. It has been my experience that if the above system testing isn't done, verified and approved by some independent validation unit (quality control, internal audit, outside consultants, or similar), then we have a problem in 60 percent of the implementations.

Finally, a robust "release management" process, in addition to strong change management practices, should be the ultimate goal. Rigorous practices for building, testing and issuing IT changes have a broad impact on individual IT results and overall performance of an organization. Therefore, while implementing a comprehensive change management program is important, establishing a strong release management process as well is strongly recommended.

IT audit guidance

The IT Compliance Institute has published an IT audit checklist covering change management. This paper, *IT Audit Checklist: Change Management*, supports an internal audit of the organization's change management policies to verify compliance and look for opportunities to improve efficiency, effectiveness and economy. The paper includes advice on assessing the existence and effectiveness of change management in project oversight, development, procurement, IT service testing and IT operations; guidance for management and auditors on supporting change management; and information on ensuring continual improvement of change management efforts.

Are your technology changes well managed? I believe it's time to find out – *refer to Chapter 9 for more information on (and how to access) the IT audit checklist.*

Auditing information security: are you protected?

I recently read that many people worry about accidental death, particularly in ways that are very frightening: poisonous snakes or spiders, or even alligator attacks. This same article noted that based on official death statistics, the vast majority of people actually die from chronic health causes: heart attacks, obesity and other ailments that result from poor attention to long-term personal fitness.

In 2003, accidental deaths in the United States numbered around 100,000; chronic health-related deaths were more than 2.4 million. The point of this article, of course, was that people must focus their attention in the correct places when they consider what would most influence the quality of their lives. Exactly the same issue exists at organizations where the Board and management must ensure they build and sustain the long-term health of the organization. This concept also applies when auditing information security. Does your information security program need to go to the gym, change its diet, or perhaps both? I recommend you audit your program to find out.

The internal audit department should evaluate the company's health – that is, internal auditors should evaluate the critical functions of the organization for long-term sustainability. Do risk management efforts identify and focus on the right risks? Does senior management encourage the right level of risk taking within defined tolerances? Is the *status quo* challenged regularly? Is the company considered a good place to work? What could bring the organization down, and are measures in place to prevent or reduce that possibility (say, by running continuity scenarios and exercises)?

To that end, internal audit should have regular talks with management and the Board regarding the organization's information security efforts. Are management and staff anticipating tomorrow's requirements? Is the organization building "muscle" for critical security activities (policy development, awareness and education, security monitoring, security architecture, secure code development, research and development, and so forth)? Is there a comprehensive security planning process and program? Is there a strategic vision, mission, strategic plan or tactical plan for security that is integrated with the business? Can the security team and management sustain them as part of conducting day-to-day business? Is the information security program focused on the critical information protection needs of the organization, or is it worried about the accidents? Are the results of security efforts reported regularly?

Evaluating security

The exact role of internal audit regarding information security varies widely among companies, but it always provides a significant opportunity for internal audit to deliver real value to the Board and management. Internal auditors should play an important role in ensuring that information security efforts have a positive effect on an organization and protect the organization from harm. Why worry so much about information security?

Consider some reasons why organizations need to protect their information:

- **Availability**: Can your organization ensure prompt access to information or systems to authorized users? Do you know if your critical information is regularly backed-up and can be easily restored?
- **Integrity of data and systems**: Are your board and audit committee confident they can rest assured that this information has not been altered in an unauthorized manner and that systems are free from unauthorized manipulation that could compromise reliability?
- **Confidentiality of data**: Can you tell your customers and employees that their non-public information is safe from unauthorized access, disclosure or use? This is a significant reputational risk today!
- **Accountability**: If information has been compromised, can you trace actions to their source?

An audit of information security can take many forms. At its simplest, the auditors will review the information security program's plans, policies, procedures and key new initiatives, and hold some interviews with the key stakeholders. At its most complex, a large internal audit team will evaluate almost every aspect of the security program and even do intrusion testing. This diversity depends on the risks involved, the assurance requirements of the Board and executive management, and the skills and abilities of the auditors. For example, if the organization is undergoing extensive change within its IT application portfolio or IT infrastructure, that would be a great time for a comprehensive assessment of the overall information security program (likely best just before or just after the changes). If last year's security audit was positive, perhaps a specialized audit of a particular activity or an important e-commerce application would be useful. The audit evaluation can, and most times should, be part of a long-term (read: multi-year) audit assessment of security results. Defining the audit goals, objectives and scope for a review of information security is a vital first step. The organization's information security program and its various measures cover a broad span of roles, processes and technologies and, just as importantly, support the business in numerous ways. Security really is the cardiovascular system of an organization and must be working at all times. Firewalls, monitoring technologies, encryption software, network architectural design, desktop asset management, identity management solutions, high-availability solutions, change management and change auditing systems, logical access control solutions – the list of security systems, technologies and processes used is almost endless. The planning phase of the audit needs to ensure the proper focus and depth of audit evaluation. Internal auditors need to determine the level of their involvement, the best audit approach to take during the audit planning, and the skill sets they'll need.

The decision about how aggressively internal auditing should evaluate information security should be based on an audit risk assessment and include factors such as: risk to the business of a security compromise of a critical asset (information or system); the experience of the information security management team; size and complexity of the organization and the information security program itself; and the level of change in the business and in the information security program. Information security standards dictate that information security controls should be selected in the light of an asset-level risk assessment.

Aggregating assets is sensible when one is dealing with a group of like assets exposed to the same risks ("risk" being defined as the likelihood of an identifiable threat exploiting a specific vulnerability).

Auditing information security should, therefore, include auditing the organization's risk assessment process and the appropriateness of the controls selected, implemented, monitored, reviewed and updated as a result of the risk assessment.

Moving to continuous improvement

Like most audits, audit of an information security program will generally involve three phases: planning, fieldwork and reporting. Information security programs, however, come in many shapes and sizes, so the audit of information security must be flexible and risk based. The audit should encourage the organization to build strength, endurance and agility in its security program efforts.

During the planning phase, the internal audit team should ensure that all key issues are considered, that the audit objectives will meet the organization's assurance needs, that the scope of work is consistent with the level of resources available and committed, that coordination and planning with IT and the information security staff has been effective, and that the program of work is well understood by everyone involved. It is important that the audit scope be defined using a risk-based approach to ensure that priority is given to the more critical areas. Less critical aspects of information security can be reviewed in separate audits at a later date.

In the fieldwork phase, the auditor analyzes the various components of the information security program based on the scope identified in the planning phase. Among some of the important questions that may be asked in a typical audit are:

- Does the information security program reflect the risks and complexity of the organization?
- Is the program actively investigating and implementing new ways of protecting the organization from harm based on threat trends?
- Is there an active education and awareness effort, so that management and staff understand their individual roles and responsibilities?
- Are the security measures and controls regularly tested for operational effectiveness, and are corrective actions occurring?
- Is performance being measured and reported to stakeholders?
- How does the organization's security compare with other well-run similar organizations?

Audit tests could include: reviewing program plans and budgets; interviewing key executives; looking at security training materials; reviewing management test plans to evaluate operating effectiveness of security efforts and their results; reviewing management's communications to employees regarding the importance of security to the organization and how it contributes to long-term success; and studying the support and trends for performance reporting. On the more technical side, try assessing intrusion detection practices, testing of physical and logical access controls, and using specialized tools to test security mechanisms and potential exposures. The evaluation of business continuity and disaster recovery efforts could be considered as well.

The bottom line: Internal auditors should be the company doctor:

- completing regular physicals that assess the health of the organization's vital organs and verify that the business is taking the necessary steps to stay healthy and secure
- encouraging management and the Board to invest in information security practices that contribute to sustainable performance and ensuring the reliable protection of the organization's critical assets.

Scoping out an audit of privacy programs

Any corporation of any size today must worry about privacy and information security. Protecting sensitive information has always made good sense, but most developed nations now have laws that restrict some uses of at least some types of data. European countries regulated personal data protection in the mid-1990s. Canada's Personal Information Protection and Electronic Documents Act (PIPEDA) has been on the books since 2001. Asian and Latin American countries have also passed privacy laws. While the US has not implemented a national privacy law, 44 states have their own such laws. The consequences for infractions can be draconian. In short, ensuring that sensitive information is secure is one of the most important jobs internal auditors have.

Information security supports privacy

Put simply, *privacy* is the confidential preservation of personal and proprietary information that shouldn't be available without the data subject's explicit permission or entitlement. Although companies often limit privacy practices to customer data, the same protection principles can – and usually should – also apply to *other* kinds of sensitive information, such as employee and business-partner information, proprietary business data, intellectual property and many other types of information. Since sensitive data crops up in virtually every corporate function a business has, companies need to take a deep, critical look at the many business needs and legal requirements that affect the ways they collect, use, transmit and store various types of information.

The fundamental restrictions on consumer-oriented information can usually be considered a good "baseline control" for all the other privacy and security considerations a company has. That said, a company's specific policies and procedures for data breach notifications, collection limitations, consumer control over data, and other controls will depend on the industry, business practices, customer expectations and other factors. To respond to the increasing number and level of threats, companies must provide concrete assurance of strategic and comprehensive privacy programs that incorporate managerial, operational and technical controls. What many think of as information protection – primarily technical controls, such as account access management, encryption, and secure software development protocols and anti-virus software – is just one piece of this complex puzzle. Organizations also need to implement and regularly assess other, generally non-technical, controls.

Getting started on an audit

Although companies often conceptually and procedurally segregate privacy and information security, the practices are two sides of the same coin and neither can be effectively evaluated in a vacuum. Privacy objectives and obligations provide direction, scope, relevance and priority for information security controls. Information security provides the confidentiality, availability and integrity of sensitive information that underpins privacy assurance.

What auditors want to see

Auditors want to see the following:

- sound, proactive managerial practices, including planning, direction, frequent operational monitoring and regular reporting
- a good balance between strategic and tactical goals for both control objectives and operational results
- decisions and actions based on facts, not assumptions or habits
- well-documented policies, standards and procedures
- documented roles, responsibilities, accountability and command chains; workforce development; assurance that staff cuts and that absences will not compromise controls; and policies for secure staff turnover
- staff awareness, training and professional development
- consistent compliance with policy and procedures by both staff and managers
- functional, reliable technical controls
- management and staff being able to recognize and respond to emerging threats and changing risk factors.

Accordingly, privacy audits tend to focus on organizational processes: how information is used; whether those uses are legal, ethical and supportable from the perspective of the company's relationship with its customers; and how the organization communicates with customers and other entities about its privacy practices. Information security assessments also evaluate managerial oversight and operational practices, but they tend to be more technically intensive than privacy audits. Auditors look at automated processes for user authentication, systems access, technology configuration and other security measures within information systems. Management must support this evaluation with functional tests, evidence of system performance and technical documentation.

A typical privacy audit scope includes an evaluation of policies, standards, procedures and plans for data protection; incident response and customer consent management; roles, responsibilities and accountability related to privacy and data protection; data collection and use in relation to intended purposes, legal constraints and customer consent; employee awareness and education programs, as well as employee hiring, transfer and termination controls; control monitoring and reporting; and existing practices benchmarked against good practices for information security. Privacy and security audits should generally be performed annually, and sometimes more frequently. Within the scope mentioned above, auditors will generally evaluate controls under three major groupings.

Management controls encompass the managerial programs, support and foundations for effective, efficient privacy and data protection programs. In general, management control audits assess whether: privacy and security policies and procedures have been implemented, performance metrics are documented and performance is measured, controls are supported by adequate budgets, staff and other resources, and a continuous improvement program is in place and operates effectively. Has the organization required personnel to confirm their understanding of privacy policies and procedures before authorizing access to sensitive information?

Operational controls encompass operational processes in which privacy and data protection are factors, including how the organization oversees privacy and data protection, and the measurement and improvement of control effectiveness. In general, operational control audits assess whether: rules and requirements exist and are documented; controls operate well; employee and managerial actions are in alignment with regulatory requirements; operational processes support privacy and security objectives; and appropriate managers regularly review key performance reports and operating results. One key question to ask: does the organization periodically perform a risk analysis, to determine the potential material harm that could result from the unauthorized manipulation of information and IT systems that support the operations and assets of the organization? That assessment should include potential impacts on:

- brand value
- stock value and investor relationships
- legal liability and regulatory sanctions
- customer and class-action litigation
- customer and employee loyalty and trust
- revenue from customers, business partners and other relationships.

The assessment should also consider and document a worst-case scenario for the compromise, corruption or misuse of the entire set of data, subject to the assessment.

Technical controls encompass systems and automated functions that support privacy and data protection goals. Technical controls address risk inherent in system design, access and operation, as well as risks inherent in the business processes facilitated by organizational technologies.

Be proactive

As in all audits, it cannot be overstressed that managers, not auditors, are responsible for defining and implementing solutions to issues found in the audit. Auditors can help management to understand identified risks, best practices and common privacy and data protection frameworks. Auditors cannot – and should not attempt to – dictate management's response to known deficiencies. Such an effort would undermine auditor independence and degrade the value of the audit process itself.

Educating staff leads to improved IT security

In today's business environment, information security and protection of information assets are vital to the long-term success of all organizations. Information is the lifeblood of corporations and a vital business asset. IT systems connect every internal department of a company and connect the whole company to myriad suppliers, partners, customers and others on the outside, too. Still, problems with IT – from system failure to data breaches, to improperly altered applications – happen almost every day. Security breaches in particular can be disastrous for a company. Most companies do not adequately address the primary cause of IT security breaches: human error. In this section, I explore how workforces should be educated about IT security and how to determine whether they "get it."

Rating your IT security program

How do you get started figuring out how well your company performs on information security? This checklist will get you started:

- Has your organization implemented a comprehensive information security program?
- Does your organization have robust and effective information security policies, procedures and controls? Are they enforced?
- Does management promote an ethical culture? Would you say your workforce follows management's lead to create a strong ethical culture?
- Does the information security program reflect the risks and complexity of the organization? Are risk assessments occurring?
- Does the program actively identify new ways of protecting the organization from harm based on emerging threats?
- Are the security measures and controls regularly tested for operational effectiveness, and are corrective actions occurring?
- Is your information security and privacy training effectiveness measured throughout the entire training lifecycle?

- Is performance being measured and reported to senior leadership and other key stakeholders?
- How does the organization's security compare with other well-run similar organizations?
- Was your security program evaluated in the past 12 to 18 months?

If you answered "yes" to all the above questions, congratulations, you're well on your way to an effective and sustainable information security program. Now, answer four more questions that will help move you to the head of the class:

- Does your program include ongoing security awareness?
- Do appropriate staff members get security education appropriate for the jobs they perform?
- Do members of the management team and workforce understand what good security practices are? How do you know?
- Are you assessing and measuring the results of your security education and awareness efforts?

The role of internal auditors

An effective internal audit function improves the company's ethical culture and control environment, both overtly through its audit work and in a more general sense by promoting good practices. Internal audits of information security awareness can provide valuable feedback to management and the Board about where overall performance can be improved, which then also contributes to more effective information security program results – definitely a win-win.

Audit work should include evaluating the organization's various security education and awareness efforts. If management and staff are not being regularly informed of emerging threats and risks, how can security be properly implemented on a sustainable basis?

An audit should compare good security practices to what is currently happening within the organization and review the results too. In other words, is quality training being provided, and is real learning happening?

Staff involvement

Education is the formal training class that a system administrator might attend to learn how to better apply Microsoft® profiles to control changes to the desktop.

Awareness is the program that a company puts in place to remind employees, through repetitive procedures (and at least an annual update in person) of policy, procedures that support policy, and practices they must know to comply with company policy. Awareness is both formal and informal. "Formal" is the 20-minute annual awareness session, whereas "informal" comprises excerpts in company newsletters, security awareness e-mails and general event reminders. A good method to deliver that security awareness message to the workforce is first to educate them on the actions they can take to protect themselves personally from the issues that face individuals today. These include such things as identity theft, phishing attacks and proper precautions to take when sharing personal information online. Provide this information in the training sessions; make the process personal. More security education and awareness practices are presented below.

- **Practice 1**: Regularly provide updated threat information to management and staff. Some common concerns today include: password theft, laptop theft, infected e-mails, "shoulder surfing" and dumpster diving. With clear communication channels that allow everyone to be more informed on the latest threats, and changes in previous threats, it encourages the workforce to be better prepared and to consider new security measures where beneficial. Many times, an educated and motivated workforce is your best defense.
- **Practice 2**: Explain the possible consequences of security incidents in business terms. Your company or its workers could endure identity theft, equipment theft, loss of productivity, loss of competitive advantage, increased staff turnover, penalties due to compliance fines, loss of reputation, loss of data, and eroded customer confidence. While the list is long, the workforce absolutely must know what the effects on the business could be. By making it "personal" and demonstrating the possible hit to operations, increased support for good information security practices can be "reinforced."
- **Practice 3**: Provide comprehensive, role-based courses to select management and staff that require the latest knowledge regarding good security practices. Here, the issue is ensuring that an investment in skills and staff competencies is happening on a regular basis. There is nothing worse than not knowing something you think you do know.
- **Practice 4**: Regularly provide best-practice information for various IT security and IT management processes. Some important processes include: patch and change management, configuration management, security design and architecture, fraud prevention and detection,

physical security – and there are many more. Explain not just the "how," but the "why" of various security processes and procedures to staff. A wise first step is to focus on educating "the influencers" of your management and staff ranks, and then let them set the example for the rest.

- **Practice 5**: Complete periodic surveys of management and staff. This is to assess how well they understand the information security policy, procedures and controls, as well as to identify key opportunities for improvement. Communication is a two-way street, and if you never assess staff competency you'll never know how well your staff development efforts are going. Surveys are a low-key method of finding out what's on the minds of people and what training issues need to be addressed.

While these steps aren't necessarily inexpensive and your company will always have limits to its education budget, over the long haul these are low-cost investments with a high-benefit payoff: peace of mind about your information security.

Regular evaluations

Setting clear expectations and defining everyone's responsibilities for IT security is half the battle. Being diligent in your efforts to be sure the workforce understands the organization's expectations and their roles and responsibilities is the other half. To implement proper security, you need an articulate policy, it must be enforced and violators must be investigated and punished when necessary. Management must understand that it has a responsibility to design and implement information security education and awareness activities, including the monitoring of those results. Management and staff need to be assigned security responsibilities, and their compensation increases should include assessing their security "performance," as well as the more traditional criteria for setting pay. Holding management and staff accountable for their performance regarding information security is key to effective security. (It's called ensuring "consequences" for people's "actions.")

Awareness should take multiple forms, such as company newsletters or impromptu forums. The effectiveness of any such effort also depends on the tone set by senior management.

The best defense against security incidents and failure is having a "motivated" and educated management and workforce to support your organization's IT security standards. Many things can happen due to lack of awareness and education, from lost customer confidence to lost customers, as well as lower stock prices, lawsuits, bad publicity, and more. The list is endless. Building awareness of information security takes time, resources and energy, but without question, it's worth it.

Auditing records management

In a column at the start of 2007, I contended that auditing records management programs should be one of your top dozen priorities for 2007. This section explores that important subject in more detail. Auditing a records management program in many ways should follow the traditional program audit. That is to say, review the program's goals and objectives; assess what has been implemented to achieve them; identify opportunities for improvement; evaluate program performance; and report your audit analysis and recommendations. In particular, however, records management includes maintaining your compliance records. Many companies have compliance policies, but do not understand why this area is so important; that is, they do not monitor compliance and record the effectiveness of that compliance. Such sloppy recordkeeping can leave companies exposed. Waiting until a lawsuit strikes is not a good time to determine if your records management policy is being followed.

Engagement planning

Defining the audit objectives is the first and one of the most critical steps in setting the audit direction. This step should include understanding the company policy, goals and objectives for records management and understanding who owns the process, how compliance is monitored and how best practices are determined. This step also defines the level of assurance the Board and management will be provided. Internal audit teams should discuss that with management and the Board, to understand just how much assurance they want. The audit should also review both paper records and electronic records, as each have different risk profiles, and you'll need to explore the assurances wanted for each. Some possible audit objectives include:

- Determine whether the records management program is documented, in place, and appropriately resourced to meet the organization's needs.
- Determine whether the program is in keeping with current good practice based on the size and complexity of the organization.

- Determine whether any other audit objectives as needed by the Board, a board committee, or management, are being met.

The nature of the organization affects the nature of the audit. A large multinational organization has different business issues and challenges than a small business. As such, the generic audit procedures provided below must be "customized" to fit the organization's environment and the assurance needs of the Board, management, and other stakeholders.

The general steps in the internal audit process include:

- **Step 1**: Define the scope, goals and objectives of the evaluation.
- **Step 2**: Define the organization's assurance needs.
- **Step 3**: Identify the evaluation team and skills required.
- **Step 4**: Develop the evaluation plan.
- **Step 5**: Perform an evaluation of the design's adequacy.
- **Step 6**: Perform an evaluation of operational effectiveness.
- **Step 7**: Communicate evaluation results and ensure follow-up to address issues.

The planning phase defines the components of the audit project plan and includes developing the:

- purpose of the audit
- description of the program (i.e. the entity to be audited)
- audit scope and scope exclusions
- audit objectives and approach
- high-level audit schedule and detailed audit timeline
- necessary skills and the internal audit team
- other resources as required.

Engagement testing

The audit itself can involve a wide range of tests. For example, look at the consistency and integration of records management among business units within the enterprise. Do they all follow the same policies? Do they all train compliance officers in the business units with the same goals and policies in mind? Do they all produce the same sort of measurable results? Other avenues of testing might be to explore:

- coordination between the central office and individual business units on records management
- confidentiality of the information handled by the records management staff
- the use of emerging technologies and other best practices in meeting today's (or better yet, tomorrow's) records management needs, for example, new rules for e-discovery in civil litigation impose tough new expectations that companies will be able to identify and procure relevant records in short order: Can you do that?
- coordination between records management overseers and other departments that might need access to the company's whole realm of data, such as the legal department putting a "hold" request on certain e-mail messages relevant to a lawsuit.

The audit team should evaluate the records management efforts regarding its effect on organizational performance, scope and strategy, structure and resources, management of policies and training, and ongoing improvement efforts. The auditor should ensure there is an up-to-date understanding of the records retention requirements of all localities where the auditor operates. For example, can documents be retained in electronic form? Special attention should be given to the approvals for destruction of documents. Special attention (perhaps very special attention, depending on your industry or company history) should also be given to the retention of documents that are or may be involved in litigation.

Engagement reporting

Among the primary purposes of internal auditing is to provide the Board and management with objective assessments about the design and operation of management practices, control systems and information. To accomplish this objective, internal audit must effectively communicate audit conclusions and recommendations. Throughout the audit, the internal auditor should discuss findings and potential recommendations with management. This helps to ensure that the auditor has considered pertinent information when forming conclusions and provides an opportunity for the internal auditor and management to develop effective solutions for identified deficiencies.

At the end of the audit, this informal communication process is formalized through closing/exit meetings and written reports. The reporting phase of the audit project includes debriefing management, drafting the audit report, issuing initial and subsequent drafts, reviewing management action plans, preparing the summary report for the audit committee, and distributing the final audit report. Put another way, tell them what you did, what you found and what management intends to do going forward.

A records management program must meet the organization's needs and the growing regulatory requirements. Compliance requirements are becoming a greater driver and people are not investing to keep up with the risk. Auditing the program provides an opportunity to complete a comprehensive review of today's program and provide management with an analysis of the key opportunities for improvement. Management and auditors must survey emerging practices constantly, to ensure their organizations are adapting new and better practices regularly.

For many industries as a whole, and for pieces of virtually all industries (such as the tax department), records retention and retrieval is a legal requirement; you want to ensure the organization is meeting these requirements. Finally, for most organizations, how and when you destroy records is vital. Think of Arthur Andersen, and remember: record destruction should be a part of every records management audit.

How to audit business continuity programs

Being able to continue critical business functions while responding to a major disaster, and then to return to normal operations efficiently and cohesively afterward, is a critical success factor for all organizations. Effective business continuity (BCP) and disaster recovery (DR) programs are vital and have become a necessary cost of doing business. They must receive adequate attention and support from management, if the company is to survive and remain competitive in a post-disaster situation. The purpose of these programs is to prepare the organization to cope more effectively with major disruption. Program managers plan possible responses in advance of the actual incident(s), rather than simply responding in the heat of the moment. This planning increases the quality and consistency of the response, regardless of the person who executes the plan. The programs must cope with a wide variety of potential incidents, from man-made disasters, such as power-grid or other critical infrastructure failures to natural disasters, such as hurricanes, floods or fires.

Simple incidents also can have huge consequences, so don't under plan; for example, expect that your staff won't make it to work due to an ice storm. It is an unfortunate fact of life that, despite our best efforts, some disasters are simply unavoidable.

The quality of an organization's response to such a crisis can make the difference between its survival and its demise. Because the BCP and DR efforts are so important, and should fit hand-in-glove, I will talk about effective audits of both as one cohesive unit.

Internal auditing's role in BCP and DR

Internal audits of the BCP and DR programs are highly recommended. The Board and management need assurance regarding the effectiveness of those efforts. They want to know that the DR plan will work when needed, that the investments in BCP and DR are obtaining good value and that a disaster will not bring the business to its knees. An independent assessment of the BCP and DR programs by internal audit can provide objective feedback that helps ensure the programs are adequate to prevent a business failure. Think about it: while everyone has focused on the requirements of Sarbanes-Oxley for almost five years, have your DR and BCP efforts kept pace with today's new challenges and expanding requirements? Have an answer, because your board is increasingly likely to ask. Exactly how internal audit departments should interact with BCP and DR programs varies widely among companies. With the right approach, audit can deliver real value to the Board and executive management, by objectively assessing whether the program provides effective coverage to protect the organization from harm when a significant disaster occurs.

An audit of the BCP and DR program can take many forms. At its simplest, auditors can conduct a quick "BCP/DR health check," reviewing the plans and interviewing key stakeholders. At its most complex, the audit team can analyze almost every aspect of the program, evaluate the risk-based planning, observe BCP/DR tests, assess the completeness of the business-impact analysis, and so forth. The type and the extent of auditing performed depends on the risks involved, management's assurance requirements and the availability of audit resources. External specialist resources may be useful on occasion. The auditors might participate as formal observers in mock drills or review the program's documentation and assess its comprehensiveness and completeness. Your options are numerous.

Internal auditors normally will review what has been planned and achieved against management's expectations, and in comparison to generally accepted best practices in the field. This is where audit objectivity comes to the fore: the auditors have a legitimate purpose to assess whether management's expectations are reasonable and sufficient, given the level of risk to the organization and in relation to other similar organizations. The following advice covers the main phases of any audit: scoping, planning, fieldwork, analysis and reporting. BCP and DR programs, however, come in many shapes and sizes, so clearly the specific details of any given audit will vary according to the situation.

Audit scoping phase

As with any audit, defining the goals and objectives for a review of the BCP and DR programs is the auditor's first task. Scoping is best conducted on the basis of a rational assessment of the associated risks. The following aspects are generally worth considering when scoping a BCP and DR audit:

- **Overall program governance**: How are the programs managed? Are they given appropriate strategic direction and investment? (That is, does the organization place sufficient emphasis on BCP and DR?) Are suitable sponsors and stakeholders involved, representing all critical parts of the organization? Do they take sufficient interest in the programs, demonstrating their support through involvement and action? Moreover, most importantly, who is accountable for their success or failure?

- **Ongoing program management**: A critical success factor in every BCP and DR effort is the way in which the programs are planned and driven to ensure that they meet objectives, despite the organization's inevitable competing priorities. Does program management balance consideration of the many conflicting priorities managers face with the critical need that corporate resiliency efforts be appropriate? This is not a once-a-year exercise anymore; being prepared is an ongoing, day in and day out effort.

- **Definition and accuracy of the BCP and DR objectives**: Have the programs' requirements been clearly and fully defined by management? Has a comprehensive business-impact analysis been completed? Is it regularly updated?

- **Coverage of the BCP and DR plans**: Have all the critical business processes been identified and suitable plans prepared? Do the plans take sufficient account of the need to maintain or recover the supporting infrastructure (IT servers and networks, for example)? Are the plans reasonably "tidy" or are they cluttered with non-essential processes, systems and activities? Are significant outsourced activities adequately covered? Do they need validation as well?

- **Management of any system or process changes**: Inevitably, changes will be required to implement BCP and DR arrangements. Is change management managed effectively to provide the best assurance that changes are tracked and addressed within the live and DR environments?

- **Robustness of the BCP and DR**
  o **DR testing processes**: Program managers need to demonstrate the organization's preparedness, build management confidence, and most importantly, strengthen the organization's BCP and DR capabilities; Is "people participation" identified, approved and tracked to provide the best assurance that the drills and tests are actually attended, and that those results meet your BCP and DR objectives?
  o **Plan maintenance**: How is the change-management process that keeps the plans up to date governed, even as the organization changes? Are roles and responsibilities allocated within the organization for developing, testing and maintaining BCP and DR plans?

o **BCP and DR procedures**: Consider the procedures and associated training, guidelines, and so forth to make managers and staff familiar with the process to follow in a disaster.

In addition to defining what aspects fall within the audit's scope, equally important is that management and the Board clarify any aspects that are out of the scope – particularly any important considerations that, for one reason or another, are not going to be covered at this time (say, perhaps because they will be audited separately). A natural part of the scoping phase is to identify one or more management sponsors for the audit. Audits are conducted for the benefit of the company's management, rather than for audit's own purposes, so it is important to know who will receive, accept and act upon the final audit report. Their overt support for the audit can make audit's job much easier, such as by engaging and gaining the involvement of suitable auditees.

Audit planning phase

Having defined the scope, the audit team needs to plan the audit within the constraints of available resources from the audit department and from the business as a whole. Resourcing decisions are largely risk based, taking account of factors such as the program management's experience, the level of management involvement in the program efforts, the size and complexity of the program, and the potential effects on the organization if the program fails.

The availability of suitable auditors is, of course, a prerequisite. Audit teams combining business and IT auditors are recommended wherever possible, since BCP and DR span both fields of expertise.

This is also a good time for the auditors to identify and contact the primary auditees. Securing their assistance with the audit fieldwork is easier if they have an opportunity to comment on the timing and nature of the work required – provided that the audit department's independence and objectivity are not unduly compromised in the process! The audit approach also needs to be decided during the audit planning. For instance, will it be feasible to review all BCP and DR plans, or is it necessary to sample the plans? If so, on what basis will the sample be selected? Should auditing of BCP and DR efforts be separate and distinct audits? (For many organizations this could make sense, as they are both important activities worthy of a focused and comprehensive review.) Does auditing of outsourced activities and related BCP and DR plans need to be completed?

Most auditors generate an audit checklist at this stage, converting the agreed audit scope into a structured series of audit tests that they plan to conduct. Styles vary, but the most useful checklists aim to guide (rather than constrain) the auditors, since the extent of the audit testing required depends somewhat on what is found. Researching what's available regarding an audit program is, as always, recommended. In addition, before fieldwork commences, audit management should review the audit plans and checklists to ensure that all of the key issues identified in the scope have been given sufficient consideration to satisfy management's assurance needs.

Audit fieldwork phase

In this phase of the audit, the auditors examine the BCP and DR program based on the goals and methods decided upon in the earlier phases. BCP helps the organization to survive a disaster by keeping critical business processes operating during the crisis, whereas DR restores the other less-critical processes following the crisis. Audit testing during the fieldwork phase gathers sufficient evidence to assess whether the program is able to meet these two fundamental requirements.

Audit tests of a BCP and DR program may include the following:

- interviewing key stakeholders and participants in the program
- reviewing business-case-, planning- and IT-related documents
- more or less detailed reviewing of individual BCP and DR plans, checking that they are complete, accurate and up to date, for example, testing a sample of the contact details for key players to confirm whether their phone numbers are correct
- looking for defined recovery times and whether there is evidence that they can be met
- examining training materials, procedures, guidelines, and so forth, plus any management communications regarding BCP and DR situations that might occur and what employees should do
- reviewing testing plans and the results of any tests already conducted
- evaluating relevant employee preparedness and familiarity with procedures
- reviewing impact of new regulation on plan

- reviewing contractor and service provider "readiness" efforts.

Details of the tests are normally recorded in the audit checklist. They are accompanied by a file containing the corresponding audit evidence, such as annotated copies of BCP and DR plans, test results and other materials that the auditors have reviewed.

Audit analysis and reporting phase

Audit reporting is a straightforward process, at least in theory. This is where the auditors analyze the results of their tests, formulate their recommendations, prepare and finally present a formal audit report to management. In the report, the auditors explain:

- **What they set out to do**: This part of the report will introduce the risks and recap the audit scope.
- **The audit methods**: This will describe how the auditor went about meeting the objectives.
- **What they found**: This typically covers the key issues identified, if not the full gory details. Not all findings are reportable, but sometimes it helps to provide the completed audit checklist as an appendix to the report and invite management to review the audit evidence, if it wants more information.
- **The recommendations**: This will entail advice to management on how to address the issues identified.

In practice, audit reporting varies widely among organizations. It requires a careful balance between the somewhat idealistic outlook of some auditors and the realities of managing the organization with limited resources and competing priorities. There is usually a fairly involved, iterative process of drafting, reviewing and correcting the report and negotiating the details with management to reach the best possible outcome for the organization. At the end of the day, it is management – not the auditors – that is responsible for deciding which, if any, recommended improvements to the BCP and DR program they intend to make.

The audit process has the advantage of systematic collection, testing and evaluation of audit evidence by an independent, yet interested, function. The facts of the matter carry a lot of weight with management. The audit report should present the purpose and objectives of the audit, the audit approach and test performed, the key opportunities for improvement, as well as detailed findings and management's action plans. A description of the actual BCP and DR program, including its scope, mandate, role and accomplishments also would be useful in getting everyone on the same page regarding organizational investments in BCP and DR efforts.

Investment in resiliency

Auditors can bring considerable value to an organization by evaluating both IT and organizational aspects of the BCP and DR program. Because failure of the BCP and DR programs when needed is one of the highest risks that an organization can face, internal auditors' independent assessment of the program will provide value far in excess of the audit's costs. Management always should be looking for ways to improve its BCP and DR program efforts – that is, don't just wait for an audit. Involve internal audit in your ongoing program efforts, such as the design and execution of a testing exercise. Regular management "self-assessments" should be encouraged, and comprehensive testing of the program is always strongly recommended.

Companies need to take a boardroom perspective for their BCP and DR program efforts. What absolutely must be in place to ensure the organization's survival? Do you have the plans and programs in place to deal with a significant disruption to operations? (Including assigning responsibilities and accountabilities for business continuity efforts and providing the program with the necessary resources to deliver when needed.)

> **The bottom line**: Is your investment in resiliency appropriate? What measures have been implemented to track your progress? Finally, is management regularly assessing and improving the organization's "preparedness" capabilities in the event of a disaster?

The tipping point for board oversight of IT

Traditionally, and properly, a company's board of directors has focused on governing the organization; that is, the Board ensures that the right CEO is in place, that the right business strategies have been developed, that performance is reported regularly and trending properly, and that the right questions are being asked of management. The Board's agenda is truly endless, and it is absolutely critical that the Board does not micromanage the CEO, attempt to "manage" the organization, or have items on its agenda that are not focused on the long-term success of the organization. The Board should revisit its mandate periodically, reconfirming its roles and responsibilities.

We need to pose the question of what the Board's oversight role is regarding information technology. There is no one right answer to this question, it can even be said the short answer is, "It depends." Indeed, many believe it is not the purview of the Board to discuss IT strategy; the Board is there to provide oversight to management's efforts, and since IT is only a "tool" in achieving those business strategies, in general, it should not be on the Board's agenda. At the other end of the spectrum there are those who maintain that IT is the business for most organizations today, and that as IT goes, so goes the company.

Therefore, the Board needs to be informed and participate in discussions about IT investments, including the organization's IT strategies, plans and processes. Finally, there are others who believe IT or IT security will be the source of our next Enron-style corporate malfeasance, so the Board needs to be much more active with IT and IT security efforts.

Revisit, review, reconsider

My recommendation is that the Board should review and define its oversight role regarding IT. That is, the Board should understand how important the IT activities are to the organization's implementation of business strategies, what IT initiatives are critical to the organization's success, what the strengths and weaknesses of the IT management team are, and what, if any, changes should be instituted regarding the Board oversight of IT.

A basic focus of the Board is ensuring corporate viability, and protecting and increasing shareholder value. If IT is so critical today to the long-term success of the company, then the Board should provide oversight of IT. The Board should *not* get involved in day-to-day management, but it *must* maintain active oversight. IT is a key contributor to the organization's results, including the always visible financial reporting and disclosure effort – and we all know what happens with incorrect financial reporting.

A fundamental question for each organization to investigate and answer is whether board oversight of IT is a "missing piece to the puzzle" in its board governance, or if it is a non-issue for that organization. While the answer is most likely somewhere in the middle of these two extremes, it is up to the Board to decide its mandate, including its roles, responsibilities and various oversight processes. The industry involved can be a factor regarding the degree of oversight needed. Obviously, an IT company and others in the technology sector should consider having a few board directors with IT expertise. Such companies probably need greater board oversight over IT strategy and investments than others, with some even having a board-level technology committee. There are actually few industries today where IT governance is not significant, although the financial, health and technology sectors certainly require more oversight than others.

Defining the Board's IT oversight role

Why is board oversight of IT so important today? Consider:

- The growing extent that corporate productivity is now related to "intellectual capital." With IT so essential to creating organizational value, boards need to understand IT better. That isn't captured through monitoring other, more traditional, areas.

- Productivity growth statistics and estimates of how much of that growth is caused by smart use of IT. Everyone is in a competitive business, and IT can give companies a competitive advantage.

Just because the Board has not taken an active role in IT in the past or put IT on the Board agenda very frequently, that does not mean there isn't a place for the Board regarding IT. It's always better to decide the Board's role going forward than to have it dictated by the next Enron that occurs. I also believe that periodically revisiting the Board's mandate and its various committees' terms of reference is a productive activity in this never-ending effort to improve governance and organizational performance. At the end of the day, isn't that what it is all about?

The Board's governance of the company as it relates to IT will depend on the nature of the organization and also of risks, both strategic and tactical. The Board's involvement is likely to vary over time. The Board's involvement in IT should be driven in the same way as it gets involved in marketing, personnel, legal and other departments – in that there is no "automatic" involvement in IT. You must decide your board's involvement and then act to achieve it.

Governance is fundamentally about identifying and managing strategic risk to the organization, whether that's the risk of the CEO turning out to be a crook, or the business strategy itself being flawed. If the organization doesn't use IT, there's obviously no risk. If the organization has enterprise-level investment in (and dependence on) information and IT, then there is risk. It is the *scale* of the risk that determines whether or not board oversight is necessary. Small risk: who cares? Big risk, think betting the firm on a technology project, then the Board had better oversee it. The Board doesn't need to oversee day-to-day management of IT (other than perhaps agreeing the criteria for recruiting the CIO), but we might think that there are half a dozen key performance indicators that we want to see on a regular basis that tells us how well this part of the business is being managed. There is no hard and fast rule beyond managing risk; which board wants to be on duty when an IT project leads to the company going down? Crying, "We left it to management!" will be just another way of saying, "Please sue us, because we took our fees, but we just weren't paying attention."

In my view, board oversight of IT is essential. For an ever-wider range of industries, IT is too important to be left to technologists alone. That said, the Board must limit the nature of its involvement to strategic issues. The Board should not be involved in where to draw the line in each case, but it should be sure that management is aware of the need to weigh the pros and cons and make an explicit decision in each case. The decision is basically one to be made on business grounds with a proper understanding of the potential, the risks and the constraints of available technology. Too often the business dimension will not even be considered, if these decisions are left to technology experts alone. Further significant insights are provided in the resources identified at the link below – has your organization reached its tipping point?
www.accaglobal.com/members/publications/accounting_bu siness/CPD/3132156

CHAPTER 8: HEALTHCARE INTERNAL AUDITING

If your actions inspire others to dream more, learn more, do more and become more, you are a leader.

John Quincy Adams

I write a quarterly IT column for the Association of Healthcare Internal Auditors (AHIA) in their internal audit publication entitled *New Perspectives*. With permission, excerpts of the articles are presented below (the complete articles are available at the links shown).

New perspectives on healthcare risk management, control and governance

Welcome to *New Perspectives on Healthcare Risk Management, Control and Governance*, the quarterly Journal of the Association of Healthcare Internal Auditors. *New Perspectives* addresses up-to-date information, current trends and issues in the areas of financial auditing, operational auditing, medical auditing, management and consulting, and information systems auditing, as well as the healthcare industry and the auditing profession. Excerpt from the AHIA website: *www.ahia.org/audit_library/newperspectives.shtml*.

Auditing IT initiatives is a recommended quality practice[20]

Changes to a company's information technology (IT) environment, both information systems and the underlying platforms, are a source of significant operational risk for every organization. To protect its IT investment and reduce operating risk, robust change management processes are critical. The need for a positive control environment and a very unforgiving attitude regarding unauthorized IT changes by management cannot be overemphasized. Insufficiently tested IT changes should also be an unacceptable practice.

Auditing IT investment management: how aligned is IT and the business in your organization?[21]

The Holy Grail for IT has always been to be closely "aligned" with business efforts. For years business has encouraged IT to focus on delivering business priorities. At the same time IT has tried to be an integral part of business planning and align IT efforts and investments with business priorities. At the end of the day, effective IT alignment really does require the ongoing and consistent involvement of all key participants.

---

[20] www.ahia.org/audit_library/newperspectivesarchive/new_perspectives/2008/
Summer2008/TheITPerspectiveColumn_AuditingITInitiativesIsaRecommendedQualityPr
acticebyDanSwanson.pdf.
[21] www.ahia.org/audit_library/newperspectivesarchive/new_perspectives/2008/
Fall2008/TheITPersectiveColumn_AuditingITInvestmentManagement_HowAlignedisITan
dtheBusinessinYourOrganizationbyDanSwanson.pdf.

Finance needs to be high performing![22]

The finance function is strategic because it helps drive organizations to higher levels of performance by delivering information that enables key strategic decision-making. In addition to strategic planning, a well-run finance department supports sound financial management, organizational performance reporting, treasury-related activities, and financial reporting (among numerous other things).

Improve IT security: educate staff[23]

In today's healthcare environment, information security and protection of information assets are critical activities for all organizations. Information is the lifeblood of the organization and a vital business asset. IT systems connect every internal department of an organization and connect the enterprise to a myriad of suppliers, partners.

Privacy: our next organizational challenge?[24]

The reality of healthcare operations today includes oversight of an increasing volume of personal health information which must be protected. Although the protection of sensitive and personal data has always been good business strategy, implementation has often been

---

[22] www.ahia.org/audit_library/newperspectivesarchive/new_perspectives/2010/March/TheITPerspectivebyDanSwanson.pdf.
[23] www.ahia.org/audit_library/newperspectivesarchive/new_perspectives/2009/Spring2009/TheITPerspective_ImproveITSecurity_EducateStaffbyDanSwanson.pdf.
[24] www.ahia.org/audit_library/newperspectivesarchive/new_perspectives/2009/Summer2009/TheITPerspectiveColumn_Privacy_OurNextOrganizationalChallengebyDanSwanson.pdf.

tactical and opaquely managed by IT departments. New laws, rules, and contractual obligations are changing all of this and management needs to be more involved. Even as information privacy and protection objectives grow more critical and complex, they are also increasingly subject to scrutiny by both internal and external auditors.

Are your audit priorities aligned with the organization's needs?[25]

Internal audit efforts must be risk based and contribute to the long-term assurance needs of the organization and its board. A formal audit risk assessment should be completed at least annually and the results of that assessment should direct internal audit priorities.

---

[25] www.ahia.org/audit_library/newperspectivesarchive/new_perspectives/2008/ Spring2008/TheITPerspectiveColumn_AreYourAuditPrioritiesAlignedwiththeOrganizatio nsNeedsbyDanSwanson.pdf.

CHAPTER 9: IT AUDIT CHECKLISTS

An ounce of action is worth a ton of theory.

Friedrich Engels (Philosopher)

The IT Audit Checklist series

IT Audit Checklists are a T2P (Truth to Power) members-only free resource (involves a short registration). Originally published by the IT Compliance Institute, the checklists offer practical guidance and experience-based insight to help IT, compliance and business managers prepare for more successful and productive internal audits. In addition to helping you understand what auditors look for and why, IT Audit Checklists support proactive operational self-assessments. By measuring your internal processes against the managerial, operational and technical control objectives in these papers, you can uncover new opportunities for system and process improvements – and address them pro-actively: (Checklists are available on the following website: *www.t2pa.com/analysis-a-advice/expert-advice-quick-reads/174-it-audit-checklists.*)

IT Audit Checklist: Information Security

This paper supports an internal audit of the organization's information security program with guidance on improving information security practices and processes, as well as information on assessing the robustness of your organizational security efforts. The paper is intended to help IT, compliance, audit and business managers prepare for an audit of information security controls and management and, ultimately, to ensure that both the audit experience and results are as productive as possible. More than 225 specific checklist items to help you assess internal audit readiness are provided.

Key points

According to the Information Security Forum, security management is "keeping the business risks associated with information systems under control within an enterprise." Requirements for security management include:

... clear direction and commitment from the top, the allocation of adequate resources, effective arrangements for promoting good information security practice throughout the enterprise, and the establishment of a secure environment.

The information security program is a critical component of every organization's risk management effort, providing the means to protect the organization's information and other critical assets.

A well-managed business unit (and/or program) has robust plans, procedures, goals, objectives, trained staff, performance reporting and ongoing improvement efforts. The audit team will look for evidence that the information security program is well organized and well managed. The security program must also specifically mitigate risks in satisfying key business objectives, and this traceability must be clear.

Your information security audit should confirm that key risks to the organization are being identified, monitored and controlled; that key controls are operating effectively and consistently; and that management and staff have the ability to recognize and respond to new threats and risks as they arise.

Audits and reviews of your information security program and its management advance the goal of program oversight and ensure continuous improvement and success.

The information security audit's goals, objectives, scope and purpose will determine the actual audit procedures and questions that are required. This document provides a foundational IT audit checklist you can use and modify to fit your specific situation.

IT Audit Checklist: Change Management

This paper, *IT Audit Checklist: Change Management*, supports an internal audit of the organization's change management policies, in order to verify compliance and look for opportunities to improve efficiency, effectiveness and economy. The paper includes: advice on assessing the existence and effectiveness of change management in project oversight, development, procurement, IT service testing and IT operations; guidance for management and auditors on supporting change management; and information on ensuring continual improvement of change management efforts. 187 specific checklist items to help assess your internal audit readiness are provided.

What auditors want to see

Auditors like the following features:

- organized, clear and up-to-date documentation
- regular managerial analysis of operating results
- management actions based on facts and actual results

- documentation of the chain of command and roles and responsibilities, such as up-to-date organization charts and the related job descriptions
- timely investigation and clearance of reconciliation items within key accounts
- supervisory review of critical performance reports
- consistent understanding and use of policy and procedures, from senior management through frontline staff, with no substantial misunderstandings
- good management practices: planning, direction, monitoring, reporting, etc.
- a balance of short- and long-term focus, for both objectives and results
- staff development, in terms of knowledge, skills, productivity and other metrics
- an engaged workforce and management team.

IT Audit Checklist: IT Governance and Strategy

This paper, *IT Audit Checklist: IT Governance and Strategy*, supports an internal audit of the organization's IT leadership and high-level planning resources, systems and processes. The audit guide includes guidance on assessing the completeness, effectiveness and sustainability of existing IT governance and strategy; guidance on supporting effective IT leadership; and information on ensuring continual improvement of governance efforts. More than 120 specific checklist items to help you assess internal audit readiness are provided.

What auditors want to see

Audits exist to assess how well a business unit or program meets the performance goals of the organization, as dictated by the CEO, CFO, board and investors. Accordingly, the managerial goal in auditing is not simply to "make auditors happy," but to demonstrate how well operations, controls and results meet the needs of the business. During audit planning, managers help auditors to design an audit process that truly reflects business strategies and goals. Thus, the managerial response to auditors throughout the audit process – planning, testing and reporting – is for the benefit of the business, not its auditors.

Auditors exist to provide the Board and senior management with an objective, independent assessment of a business unit or program (such as information security), including what they see as key opportunities for improvement. To prepare their opinions and conclusions, auditors need to review and assess evidence of the risk management program and its performance. If auditors are able to demonstrate performance and show that accountability has been established and is working, they should produce a positive audit report.

Accordingly, auditors and managers should work to help each other reach common goals – auditors striving to earnestly, honestly and completely assess program effectiveness, and management working to help auditors make valid assessments.

IT Audit Checklist: Privacy and Data Protection

This paper supports an internal audit of the organization's regulatory, legal, contractual and reputation protection requirements to maintaining the confidentiality and integrity of sensitive information related to itself, employees, customers, business partners and other entities.

The paper includes advice on assessing the robustness of privacy controls; guidance on how management and auditors support privacy policies and procedures; and information on ensuring continual improvement of privacy practices. 270 specific checklist items to help assess your internal audit readiness are provided.

What are the benefits of information security?

An information-security management program is necessary because threats to the availability, integrity and confidentiality of the organization's information are great and, apparently, ever increasing. All companies possess information that is critical or sensitive, ranging from personal data to financial and product information and customer, brand and IP information. An information security program implements protective measures to secure corporate information.

The benefits of an effective information security program include:

- the ability to systematically and proactively protect the company from the dangers and potential costs of computer misuse and cybercrime
- the ability to make informed, practical decisions about security technologies and solutions, and thus increase the return on information security investments
- the management and control of costs related to information security

- greater organizational credibility with staff, customers and partner organizations
- better compliance with regulatory requirements for security and privacy
- implementation of best practices in risk management in regard to information assets and security.

IT Audit Checklist: Risk Management

This paper supports an internal audit of the organization's risk management program and processes. Providing guidance to improve your risk management program and to assess the robustness of your risk management efforts, the checklist is intended to help business and IT managers prepare for an audit of risk management controls, making the audit experience and results as productive as possible. 80 specific checklist items to help you assess internal audit readiness are provided.

Overview

Organizations are increasingly under pressure to identify all significant business risks they face, and to develop contingency plans and/or manage them to an acceptable level. In addition, with the expanding diversity of risks, a more formalized program of risk management has also become more commonplace, generally going under the moniker of an enterprise-wide risk management (ERM) program.

Everyone in the organization has a role in ensuring a successful ERM program, although management bears the primary responsibility for identifying and managing risk and implementing ERM with a structured, consistent and coordinated approach. Boards of directors, and their non-corporate equivalents, have an overarching responsibility for monitoring the risk program efforts and obtaining assurance that the organization's risks are being acceptably managed.

Internal auditors, in both assurance and consulting roles, contribute to ERM in a variety of ways, such as evaluating the effectiveness of – and recommending improvements to – ERM efforts. Fundamentally, the audit team provides the Board and management with an objective and independent assessment of the organization's ERM efforts, including what the audit team views as being the key opportunities for improvement.

The audit's goals, objectives, scope and purpose will determine the actual audit procedures and questions that are required, therefore, modify the "base" IT audit checklist provided to fit your specific situation. An audit of ERM should determine that the key risks to the organization are being controlled, that the key controls are operating effectively and consistently, and that management and staff have the ability to recognize and respond to new risks as they arise.

CHAPTER 10: AUDITNET® DAN SWANSON'S COLUMNS

We could all use a little coaching. When you're playing the game, it's hard to think of everything.

Jim Rohn

AuditNet® Dan Swanson's columns (the summary)

I've written a monthly internal audit column for AuditNet for several years, provided below is a summary of the various articles and highlighted resources produced from that long-term effort. For easy access to the various columns go to: *www.auditnet.org/dsarticles.htm*.

Internal auditors and fraud: a 2010 resource "keeper"

Fraud is a complicated subject and linkage to good risk management and good governance practices are, of course, critical (to reduce fraud); in fact, without the latter in place the fight against fraud is doomed to eventual failure. 60 resources you should find useful (this war has been going on for many years) are available at: *www.auditnet.org/articles/DSIA201004.htm*.

Some summer reading: from the summer of 2009

Summer is a time of recharging, of planning for the future, of preparing for the next challenge. Summer is also a time to unwind and relax and spend time with the family: *www.auditnet.org/articles/DSIA200908.htm*.

Information security management

This column was originally written as it was coming up to the 8th anniversary of 9/11. With that in mind, I was thinking it would be an excellent time to take information security to the next level.

A few simple questions to consider:

- Have you reviewed your organization's security practices?
- What are the priority improvements which need to be tackled?
- Does your board, executive management and each business unit understand their responsibilities and accountabilities?

The bottom line – be prepared is always the way to go! *www.auditnet.org/articles/DSIA200909.htm*.

Improving corporate risk management!

Has your organization completed a comprehensive review of its corporate risk management practices lately? Richard Anderson's new study regarding leading practices to adopt would be a great place to start: *www.auditnet.org/articles/DSIA200907.htm*.

Building security in (is needed)!

We need to implement effective security by building it into our IT solutions. Some resources to assist your understanding of the issues involved and recommendations to move us forward are provided in this article. Does your organization incorporate security as part of its software

acquisition process and system development life cycle (SDLC) process?
www.auditnet.org/articles/DSIA200902.htm

Making information systems work

New technology has transformed the way we interact with one another and do business. However, as systems become ever-more complex, the challenges of effective implementation are greater than ever. These are challenges to the whole of the business, not just IT, and require engagement from across the organization in the effective management and use of technology.

The "Making Information Systems Work" program considers these opportunities and challenges, engaging all sectors of the economy in the debate. It is based on three themes: 1) value: the economic case for IT investment; 2) trust: a secure environment to transfer information; and 3) standards: a sound technical basis for the exchange of information between parties.[26]

How IT governance drives improved performance[27]

Companies with high maturity IT governance programs focus efforts more on agility and supporting customer facing business initiatives than lower maturity peers. They score higher on performance measures that indicate the

---

[26] *www.icaew.com/index.cfm/route/143263/icaew_ga/en/Technical_and_Business_Topics/Thought_leadership/Making_information_systems_work/Making_information_systems_work*.
[27] *How IT Governance Drives Improved Performance*, White Paper, IT Process Institute (February 2009), available at: *www.itpi.org/home/white_papers.php*.

effectiveness of governance efforts in the areas of strategic alignment, value delivery, risk management, resource management and performance management. They also score higher on measures that gauge business "value-add" in the areas of improved information management, business process efficiency, customer retention and product enablement.

A 2008 study of 389 IT organizations in North America, the United Kingdom and Australia assessed the impact of governance practices on governance performance. This 40 page report layers high-impact practices in a three-tier maturity model that can help IT executives optimize governance improvement initiatives: *www.auditnet.org/auditnet-l%202009-03.htm*.

Privacy: our next organizational challenge?

The reality of business operations today includes an increasing oversight of data privacy and information protection. Although the protection of sensitive and personal data has always been good business strategy, implementation has often been tactical and opaquely managed by IT departments. New laws, rules and contractual obligations are changing all of this. Even as information privacy and protection objectives grow more critical and complex, they are also increasingly subject to scrutiny by both internal and external auditors.

Especially given the broad scope of sensitive data, companies need to take a deep and critical look at the many business needs and legal requirements that impact the ways they collect, use, transmit and store various types of information. Companies should always apply due care based on business needs and legal requirements.

In general, four basic categories of control are involved:

- what data may be collected and under what conditions
- how data may be stored, managed, used and transferred
- how data must be protected from unauthorized and inappropriate access
- how companies should interact with the individuals whose data they control.

www.auditnet.org/articles/DSIA200905.htm

Risk oversight leadership is needed!

In today's economy and very challenging business environment, effective risk management processes are critical. Board risk oversight is fundamental to good governance and the senior management's day-to-day management of strategic, tactical and operational risk has become hugely important, some say absolutely necessary, for long-term success.

Some questions to consider:

- Are the organization's risk management efforts appropriate to its needs?
- Has a risk management program been developed and implemented?
- How effective are the risk management efforts?
- Do we need to increase the understanding of our key risks?
- Has accountability been established (for risk management?

- What else needs to be done, i.e. have we done everything necessary?
  www.auditnet.org/auditnet-l%202009-01.htm

CERT's podcast series: security for business leaders

Practicing strong information and cybersecurity is a nonnegotiable requirement for organizations doing business today. However, building security into an existing corporate culture is a complex undertaking. This series of podcasts by CERT provides both general principles and specific starting points for business leaders who want to launch an enterprise-wide security effort, or make sure their existing security program is as good as it can be:
www.cert.org/podcast/.

Technical communications[28]

Professionals can learn by studying the work of others. Identified at the link below are leaders in the ongoing quest for concise and effective communications:
www.auditnet.org/auditnet-l%202009-06.htm.

Business continuity and disaster recovery leadership

Because a crisis is no time to exchange business cards, being able to recover from and operate during (a major disaster) is "critical to your success."

---

[28] *www.icaew.com/index.cfm/route/143263/icaew_ga/en/Technical_and_Business_Topics/Thought_leadership/Making_information_systems_work/Making_information_systems_work*.

Some questions to ponder:

- Is your business unit's business continuity plan effective?
- Is your organization's business continuity plan effective?
- Is your region's business continuity plan effective?
- Is your nation's business continuity plan effective?
- Was it worth it?

Finally, and perhaps most importantly:

- How do you know it'll all work and what can you do to make it even better?
www.auditnet.org/drp.htm.

CHAPTER 11: IT WORLD CANADA: IT SECURITY RESOURCE BLOG

We have such a tendency to rush in, to fix things up with good advice. However, we often fail to take the time to diagnose, to really, deeply understand the problem first. If I were to summarize in one sentence the single most important principle I have learned in the field of interpersonal relations, it would be this: "Seek first to understand and then to be understood"

Steven Covey

IT World Canada: IT security resource blog

I've posted numerous resource blogs to the IT World Canada website. Provided below are summaries of the various postings, while focused on IT security, numerous management subjects are also covered: *www.itworldcanada.com/blogs/security/default.aspx*.

Have you started your journey yet?

Getting IT under control is all about consistent and repeatable IT processes. Change and release management has become a defining performance factor in high performing IT shops. Significant research has also been completed which identifies the huge benefits of tackling change management "head on": *http://blogs.itworldcanada.com/security/2009/03/19/have-you-started-your-journey-yet/*.

Teaching staff to fish[29]

Do you feed your employees, or do you teach them how to fish? Do you like to swoop in and save the day? Do you see yourself as the white knight that can solve any problem or challenge?
www.itworldcanada.com/blogs/security/2009/11/20/teaching-staff-to-fish/52510/

How to think for yourself

These resource selections combine a mixture of corporate governance guidance and personal growth items. "Thinking for yourself" is one of my favorite little nuggets – and it's not often you get something priceless for free:
www.itworldcanada.com/blogs/security/2009/07/28/how-to-think-for-yourself/50672/.

The importance of internal audits

These resource selections originate from a monthly internal audit column I write for Jim Kaplan, for going on more than three years now. Each month in Jim's internal audit newsletter (*www.auditnet.org/*) I highlight leading audit and security resources to assist auditors and security practitioners:
www.itworldcanada.com/blogs/security/2009/11/06/the-importance-of-internal audits/52250/.

---

[29] "Management Matters with Mike Myatt: Teach Them to Fish", *Management Matters*, Myatt M (November 2008).

Being prepared and in control

Continuing selections from my various columns for Jim Kaplan, this item highlights resources that have a "governance" focus. In addition, I want to enforce the importance of being prepared (e.g. implementing a security-incident response capability) and being "in control" (i.e. we must have effective change management). It really is endless!
www.itworldcanada.com/blogs/security/2009/11/13/being-prepared-and-in-control/52487/.

Inside the *EDPACS* newsletter

This item highlights *EDPACS*, a long time monthly IT audit and control newsletter, now into its 37th year of publication. A variety of freely available articles from their website are presented. The annual subscription cost is very reasonable and includes online access to more than ten years of articles:
www.itworldcanada.com/blogs/security/2009/10/13/inside-the-edpacs-newsletter/52101/.

All about the IIA

These resource selections highlight IIA's long-term effort to provide leading guidance to internal auditors and risk management professionals:
www.itworldcanada.com/blogs/security/2009/10/30/all-about-the-iia/52238/.

High availability: the next challenge

"CIOs must alter their thinking about their approach to availability."

- The old paradigm is "Experience and React." Things happen, we react, the organization is affected.
- The new way of thinking must be "Anticipate and Adjust." Things still happen, but their effect is neutralized; the organization feels little or no effect: *www.itworldcanada.com/news/high-availability-the-next-challenge/128155*.

A fistful of risk management resources

This item highlights three leading risk management books as well as my three-year summary of monthly columns for AuditNet and Jim's internal audit newsletter, now into its 15th year! Finally, KARL is a very unique resource which will require hours and hours of study: *http://www.itworldcanada.com/blogs/security/2009/10/05/a-fistful-of-risk-management-resources/51979/*.

Get to know auditing

These resource selections highlight a variety of audit articles which I've had the pleasure of writing. By regularly studying (auditing) what is "in place" (our current state) and identifying what the priority improvements are (our future state) we can encourage and implement continuous improvement: *http://www.itworldcanada.com/blogs/security/2009/09/15/get-to-know-auditing/51541/*.

S&P's global regulatory framework for credit ratings

These resource selections highlight the Standard & Poor's effort to improve credit ratings assessments. The evaluation of an organization's enterprise risk-management practices is a key strategy for S&P – to improve their credit rating process. Consider encouraging your organization to strengthen their ERM practices – it would make your job easier!

www.itworldcanada.com/blogs/security/2009/09/29/s-amp-amp-p-s-global-regulatory-framework-for-credit-ratings/51550/

The book on security engineering

These resource selections focus on protecting your information, designing security into your solutions and ensuring a comprehensive assurance process is "in place." It also encourages a life-long learning philosophy by providing a summary of some leading edge sources of security professional development: *www.itworldcanada.com/blogs/security/2009/09/01/the-book-on-security-engineering/51533/*.

Improving the practice of IT

Leveraging best practice research is always useful – just make sure it applies to your organization before implementing changes. These resources focus on improving the practice of IT: *http://blogs.itworldcanada.com/security/2009/04/07/dan-security-improving-the-practice-of-it/*.

Technology does not fix process!

This post looks at resiliency, security education and awareness, risk management and "process":
www.itworldcanada.com/blogs/security/2009/08/24/tech-does-not-fix-process/51262/.

NIST's security framework

This special blog highlights the NIST publication of their *Recommended Security Controls for Federal Information Systems and Organizations* (SP800-53) guidance:
www.itworldcanada.com/blogs/security/2009/08/05/nist-s-security-framework/50677/.

Compliance, fraud and business continuity

Today's information security professionals need to study current and upcoming regulatory compliance requirements to get ahead of the curve. We also need to help protect the organization from fraud and waste and, of course, that next disaster. These resources involve leading articles and papers regarding compliance, fraud and business continuity. It really never ends!
http://blogs.itworldcanada.com/security/2009/02/20/dan-swanson-compliance-fraud-and-business-continuity/

Improving your privacy practices

Has your organization reviewed its privacy practices in the past year? Are you prepared for that next disaster? Can you respond on a timely and reliable basis in the event of a major security incident, or worse, when disaster strikes?

Some leading resources to help you become better "prepared":
http://blogs.itworldcanada.com/security/2009/02/27/dan-swanson-privacy-practices/.

The finance function

The finance function is absolutely critical to the organization's long-term success. These resources provide some excellent best practice information regarding this important corporate function:
http://blogs.itworldcanada.com/security/2009/04/13/dans-security-the-finance-function/.

Getting more resilient

These resource selections focus on process improvement and strengthening the organization's operational resiliency. Have you improved the recoverability of your critical systems in the past year? I.e. it is time you started! Finally, any time spent improving your understanding of strategy is time well spent, a couple of excellent sources of best practice are also provided:
http://blogs.itworldcanada.com/security/2009/07/21/getting-more-resilient/.

Retooling your IT security plans

These resource selections focus on implementing a solid information security program that includes a comprehensive information-security enterprise architecture:
www.itworldcanada.com/blogs/security/2009/05/28/retooling-your-it-security-plans/50654/.

Staying accountable

These resource selections focus on accountability and corporate governance – two subjects every information security professional should be comfortable talking about with every executive:
http://blogs.itworldcanada.com/security/2009/06/26/staying -accountable/.

Best practices abound

The amount of valuable information available continues to amaze me. The study, and then application, of recommended practice(s) also continues to be a huge challenge, but it is better than trying to reinvent that wheel, over and over again. I'd really welcome hearing about any leading resources regarding the successful implementation of change and application of new technologies and solutions:
http://blogs.itworldcanada.com/security/2009/01/15/dan-swanson-best-practices-abound/.

Built-in security

These resource selections focus on building security into our solutions and assessing the quality of our effort. Educating management and staff is an endless task – some resources to assist in this important activity are also highlighted:
http://blogs.itworldcanada.com/security/2009/07/06/built-in-security/.

Back to the future

Learning from the past is critical in helping prevent the repeat of past mistakes. Studying new research is important in helping to adopt new practices when available and appropriate, rather than having to wait for them to go mainstream several years later. Finally, watching for a changing business environment is also important – e.g. to prevent from being hit by fast-changing requirements. It's a tough world out there!
http://blogs.itworldcanada.com/security/2009/01/08/back-to-the-future/

From ethics to college basketball

These resource selections cover ethics, project management, psychology, leadership, and even a bit of basketball:
http://blogs.itworldcanada.com/security/2009/06/05/from-ethics-to-college-basketball/.

Keeping tabs on governance and risk

These resource selections focus on governance and risk management. Monitoring the results of your efforts is a highly recommended management practice and the lessons learned, from doing so, are invaluable:
http://blogs.itworldcanada.com/security/2009/07/13/keeping-tabs-governance-risk/.

Study the work of others

Learning from other professions has always been a fast-track way of getting ahead of the curve. Studying what others are doing is (usually) way better than trying to learn on the job. As someone once said, "better to learn from the mistakes of others – than from your own":
http://blogs.itworldcanada.com/security/2008/11/20/dan-swansons-security-resources-19/.

Continuous improvement is a priority

Process improvement involves constantly revisiting your management practices and their performance. Last year stellar performance may become the baseline this year. New technologies may totally "bypass" traditional ways of doing things, on a dime, and so constant searching for new ways of doing business has become a defining critical success factor for organizations. This post includes a diverse collection of past gems (landmark reports) and websites that are continually updated with the latest news and research:
http://blogs.itworldcanada.com/security/2008/12/18/dan%e2%80%99s-security-resource-educational-column/.

It's all about the architecture

These resource selections focus on "architecture" – the solution for most everything – and IT process improvement, the solution for everything else!
http://blogs.itworldcanada.com/security/2009/06/12/its-all-about-the-architecture/

Security audits are always useful

Auditing information security helps identify key improvement opportunities, while the study of leading audit guidance provides a better understanding of what the auditors are looking for, helping make audits more productive (a true win/win): *http://blogs.itworldcanada.com/security/2008/07/18/dan-swansons-security-resources-11/*.

Don't let change just happen

Business is about change, and Peter de Jager's change management repository[30] is one of the very best, and certainly well worth regular visits by busy professionals: *http://blogs.itworldcanada.com/security/category/business-case/*.

The Boy Scout motto is there for a reason

"How prepared is your organization?" If you have any concerns regarding the robustness of your disaster recovery, business continuity and/or your emergency management capabilities, I'd strongly recommend you check out the Canadian Centre for Emergency Preparedness (CCEP available at *www.ccep.ca*): *http://blogs.itworldcanada.com/security/2008/05/08/dan-swansons-security-resources-4/*.

---

[30] Available at: *www.technobility.com/docs/menu-managing-change.htm*.

Technology is the business

Technology is becoming the solution to every business problem. As such, we need to implement our solutions faster and more securely. Moreover, we need to continually deliver "easy to use" (i.e. intuitive) system solutions. Did I mention, our enterprise solutions also have to protect the privacy of both our organization's and our organization's clients' information?
http://blogs.itworldcanada.com/security/2008/11/03/dan-swansons-security-resources-17-2/

Study: the key to success (it's that simple)

There is an endless source of good resources to support your professional development. The intent of this column is to provide a diverse knowledge base to study from each week (six items at a time). The two significant challenges many of us face are deciding what to study and where to find the time to do so. This week's top choice is Neal Whitten's[31] timeless article regarding learning from project to project; I recommend taking his suggestions to heart as they will quickly improve your results:
http://blogs.itworldcanada.com/security/2008/07/02/dan-swansons-security-resources-9/.

Can you recover from a disaster?

These resources are focused on the challenging and closely related subjects of business continuity planning (BCP) and disaster recovery (DR) programs. Being able to recover

---

[31] *www.nealwhittengroup.com/*.

from a disaster is critical to an organization's long-term success, as something is going to happen eventually: *http://blogs.itworldcanada.com/security/2008/06/19/dan-swansons-security-resources-8/*.

An educated and motivated workforce is your best defense

Have you implemented a security education and awareness program to help educate management and staff on their security responsibilities? Have you organized a process to communicate good practice information to your workforce, particularly to the key IT specialists that are implementing new IT solutions? Have you reached out lately to your DR and BCP professionals regarding recovery processes and plans? Could your organization recover from a significant disaster? These cited resources provide guidance regarding all these issues and more!
http://blogs.itworldcanada.com/security/2008/06/05/dan-swansons-security-resources-7/

Just who is responsible for information security?

Are we learning from incidents that have occurred at other organizations? Do we leverage the research that is available from various institutions? Do we take the regulations seriously?
http://blogs.itworldcanada.com/security/2008/05/30/dan-swansons-security-resources-6-2/

Project management makes things happen

Project management helps to pull it all together. If your project management experience or expertise needs strengthening these resources are just what the doctor ordered. Neal Whitten's efforts are world class, and his project management consulting advice is sought after by numerous organizations. Learning from past experiences is always recommended and the *Early Warning Signs of IT Project Failure: the Dominant Dozen*[32] is a classic that should be read before taking on any significant IT initiative: *http://blogs.itworldcanada.com/security/2008/09/05/dan-swansons-security-resources-15/*.

Don't reinvent the wheel

These resources include a diverse collection of websites and articles I've come across over the past couple of years. Checking out different organization's views and recommended guidance helps broaden your perspective and sometimes even addresses a burning business problem back at the office: *http://blogs.itworldcanada.com/security/2008/09/26/dan-swansons-security-resources-16/*.

Don't reinvent the security wheel

There are several ongoing, long-term security efforts worth examining. The National Institute of Standards and Technology (NIST) has published hundreds of guidance documents relating to all aspects of information security

---

[32] *http://www.ism-journal.com/ITToday/projectfailure.pdf*.

over the years. Just as importantly, they consistently maintain the currency of their guidance. The Center for Internet Security (CIS) has developed dozens of consensus-based security benchmark checklists that can be used for securing various technologies commonly in place, in most organizations. CIS tools have been a worldwide standard in "hardening" various technologies. And the US Department of Homeland Security's "Build Security In (BSI)" initiative is truly amazing, it is an endless source of advice and guidance and needs to be visited frequently as new items are added regularly: *http://blogs.itworldcanada.com/security/2008/05/02/dan-swansons-security-resources-3/*.

Research complements practice, and you do need to know both

This article highlights two significant security initiatives, the CERT resiliency engineering research project and the CERT Governing for Enterprise Security (GES) initiative. I also wanted to point out some landmark security guidance (the CIAO/IIA series) with the initial "call to action" paper released at the White House on April 17, 2000. As always, I have also included a couple of miscellaneous resources too: *http://blogs.itworldcanada.com/security/2008/05/15/dan-swansons-security-resources-5/*.

Good leadership AND good management are needed

Leadership is fundamental to success. Without leaders the organization, the project and the team will certainly founder. Project management is also a core fundamental, especially to the success of IT and business

initiatives. Without the ongoing management of the complex environment IT and business initiatives operate in, projects will be late, over budget, or fail to meet client expectations – perhaps all three. These resources focus on increasing your understanding of the importance of leadership, project management and audit assurance. Each of these activities contributes significantly to the complex system we operate in:
http://blogs.itworldcanada.com/security/2008/12/11/dan-swansons-security-resources-20/.

Do you search out knowledge and wisdom?

These resources will help support your quality, strategy, knowledge management and process improvement effort. Consider sharing this leading practice information with your management and staff:
http://blogs.itworldcanada.com/security/2008/11/14/dan-swansons-security-resources-18/.

Guidance only supports practice

Recently someone forwarded me a comprehensive survey of Canadian IT professionals that indicated there was a lack of information security guidance available for IT and security professionals to follow. I strongly disagree with the point of view that more guidance is needed to operate a secure environment and implement secure systems and solutions, although certainly more papers on various challenging subjects would always be beneficial.

These resources, and many more, highlight leading security resources and initiatives that will support your efforts to improve security practices within your organization. In a series of columns, I highlight a half-dozen leading security focused resources covering various aspects of information security management.

People also learn in different ways. Some like to read, some like to hear, some like to see, some like to discuss, etc. Whichever method works for you is fine. My approach is to highlight leading resources to people and let them determine the best way to digest the knowledge and, more importantly, apply it in their professional efforts.

Finally, I have found that considering how to apply the general guidance to the specific organizational situation is one of the best ways to obtain a deep understanding of the key concepts, methods and recommendations presented by the various resources. In other words – implementing change is always the best teacher. Please share this posting with your colleagues. Good luck in your efforts to make a difference: *http://blogs.itworldcanada.com/security/2008/04/18/dan-swansons-security-resources-1/.*

CHAPTER 12: SENTINEL: THE IT GOVERNANCE NEWSLETTER

Be a collector of good ideas, but don't trust your memory. The best collecting place for all of the ideas and information that comes your way is your journal.

Jim Rohn

Sentinel archive: access link

Over the past five years I've published a monthly IT Governance newsletter entitled *Sentinel*. Each month this newsletter highlights leading resources across several management topics, including: organizational governance, IT governance, risk management and internal audit, IT audit, IT management, and finally the "Picks of the Month".

> This newsletter is available at:
> *www.itgovernance.co.uk/media/newscats.aspx?cat_id=7&title =Newsletters.*

30/06/2010 Sentinel - Edition 60 - 30 June 2010

28/05/2010 Sentinel - Edition 59 - 31 May 2010

26/04/2010 Sentinel - Edition 58 - 29 April 2010

31/03/2010 Sentinel - Edition 57 - 01 April 2010

22/02/2010 Sentinel - Edition 56 - 22 February 2010

28/01/2010 Sentinel - Edition 55 - 28 January 2010

30/11/2009 Sentinel - Edition 52 - 30 November 2009

26/10/2009 Sentinel - Edition 51 - 26 October 2009

28/09/2009 Sentinel - Edition 50 - 28 September 2009

27/08/2009 Sentinel - Edition 49 - 27 August 2009

30/07/2009 Sentinel - Edition 48 - 30 July 2009

22/06/2009 Sentinel - Edition 47 - 22 June 2009

28/05/2009 Sentinel - Edition 46 - 28 May 2009

27/04/2009 Sentinel - Edition 45 - 27 March 2009

23/03/2009 Sentinel - Edition 44 - 23 March 2009

23/02/2009 Sentinel - Edition 43 - 23 February 2009

26/01/2009 Sentinel - Edition 42 - 26 January 2009

18/12/2008 Sentinel - Edition 41 - 18 December 2008

27/11/2008 Sentinel - Edition 40 - 27 November 2008

03/11/2008 Sentinel - Edition 39 - 31 October 2008

29/09/2008 Sentinel - Edition 38 - 29 September 2008

22/08/2008 Sentinel - Edition 37 - 26 August 2008

24/07/2008 Sentinel - Edition 36 - 30 July 2008

25/06/2008 Sentinel - Edition 35 - 26 June 2008

29/05/2008 Sentinel - Edition 34 - 29 May 2008

30/04/2008 Sentinel - Edition 33 - 30 April 2008

27/03/2008 Sentinel - Edition 32 - 26 March 2008

28/02/2008 Sentinel - Edition 31 - 28 February 2008

30/01/2008 Sentinel - Edition 30 - 30 January 2008

12: *Sentinel: The IT Governance Newsletter*

28/12/2007 Sentinel - Edition 29 - 28 Dec 2007

29/11/2007 Sentinel - Edition 28 - 28 Nov 2007

05/11/2007 Sentinel - Edition 27 - 5 November 2007

26/09/2007 Sentinel - Edition 26 - 26 September 2007

29/08/2007 Sentinel - Edition 25 - 28 August 2007

28/08/2007 Sentinel - Edition 24 - 26 July 2007

27/06/2007 Sentinel - Edition 23 - 27 June 2007

30/05/2007 Sentinel - Edition 22 - 30 May 2007

30/04/2007 Sentinel - Edition 21 - 30 April 2007

27/03/2007 Sentinel - Edition 20 - 27 March 2007

21/02/2007 Sentinel - Edition 19 - 21 February 2007

29/01/2007 Sentinel - Edition 18 - 29 January 2007

17/01/2007 24743 - Edition 13 - 17 January 2007

04/01/2007 24743 - Edition 12 - 4 January 2007

CHAPTER 13: CIO CANADA: IT MANAGEMENT COLUMNS

We are so obsessed with doing that we have no time and no imagination left for being. As a result, people are valued not for what they are, but for what they do or what they have – for their usefulness.

Thomas Merton

Over the course of several years in the late 1990s I highlighted leading IT management resources of use by CIOs and other senior IT managers. The more popular columns are presented below.

Positioning the CIO for success

When it comes to IT management, sometimes nothing is as valuable as the lessons learned by those facing similar management challenges: *www.itworldcanada.com/news/positioning-the-cio-for-success/129284*.

Helping management understand IT planning

Here's an online report worthy of recommending to senior management. Entitled *Managing Information Technology Planning for Business Impact*, it is an executive-level guideline developed by the International Federation of Accountants (IFAC).[33]

Planning, projects and control

Sound IT strategic planning combined with good project management, and audit and control of IT initiatives are all important elements of an effective approach to IT development. CIOs will find the Web a fertile place to find best practices and helpful management advice in all of these areas.[34]

Time for information security management to go to war

Sun Tzu's *The Art of War* has long been required reading for military leaders. Andrew Clark has taken this masterpiece of war-fighting strategy and built an inspiring corollary that draws on the techniques and motives of the war-fighter and places them in the information warfare arena. This innovative document may change the way you view your information technology defensive posture, it is entitled *Practices for Securing Critical Information Systems: www.iwar.org.uk/cip/resources/prac.pdf.*

Taking stock of projects

Are we working on the right projects? It's always a good practice to periodically review the current project portfolio.

---

[33] Published January 1999, available at: *www.ifac.org/Members/DownLoads/ITC-Guideline_2.pdf. Also see: www.itworldcanada.com/news/helping-management-understand-it-planning/135522.*
[34] See: *www.itworldcanada.com/news/planning-projects-and-control/127387* and *www.gsa.gov/technologystrategy.*

Initiatives do tend to expand in scope, and revisiting their goals and objectives can be very productive. Consider doing a quick assessment of your shop's 10 largest projects. For any initiative that appears to be struggling ask your IT project manager to complete a brief risk assessment report. Then, sit down with the project sponsor and IT project manager and rationalize what steps, if any, should be taken to get the project back on track: *www.itworldcanada.com/news/taking-stock-of-projects/127482.*

Your online HR management checklist

The continual improvement of all management practices is fundamental for an organization to be competitive in the global economy. With the special importance on human resources, HR management practices are near the top of the list when it comes to staying ahead of the pack. For example, knowledge workers need to be motivated; managers need to be leaders; training needs to be just in time; and the list goes on. Various "best practice" online documents and websites provide a variety of tools and techniques to consider, making your job easier and increasing the impact of your efforts: *www.itworldcanada.com/news/your-on-line-hr-management-checklist/133923.*

Towards effective IT governance

IT governance is a critical issue for all organizations, particularly with the rapid increase in competition worldwide. One of the constant challenges facing every CIO is proving the contribution of their information services function. In addition, delivering IT and information management (IM) services that are effective and a "value-add" to the organization is an ongoing necessity.

One of the ways CIOs can make their organizations more effective is by establishing a strong IT governance framework. Senior IT management needs to develop the management processes whereby executive management and business unit management are challenged and encouraged to participate in ensuring that:

- there is executive management buy-in and involvement in all IT initiatives
- IT priorities are linked with business objectives and goals
- there is a joint effort in the effective organizational application of information technology.

www.itworldcanada.com/news/towards-effective-it-governance/133564

CHAPTER 14: KEEPING OUR KIDS SAFE!

You will never find time for anything. If you want time you must make it.

Charles Buxton

Some great resources to help keep our kids safe are provided below.

Make a difference!

www.teachermovie.com

The Wired Kids website

This is an excellent site about safe surfing, anti-bullying, etc. Wired Kids also form the basis of a group that works in schools – Teenangels – kids teaching kids about Internet safety and etiquette: *www.wiredkids.org/*.

A call to action: be a cybersecure kid!

Securing your personal computer at home plays a crucial role in protecting our nation's Internet infrastructure. You'll find simple steps, practices and resources to learn the basics on how to teach your children to stay safe on the Internet.

This website gives you the information needed to secure your computer. You'll find practices on how to safeguard your system, a self-guided cybersecurity test, educational materials and other Internet resources, as well as valuable information from supporting organizations: *www.staysafeonline.org/*.

The National Child Exploitation Coordination Centre

The National Child Exploitation Coordination Centre (NCECC), is an integral part of Canada's National Police Services and was created to help protect children from online sexual exploitation: *www.rcmp-grc.gc.ca/ncecc-cncee/index-accueil-eng.htm*.

The National Center for Missing & Exploited Children

The National Center for Missing & Exploited Children (NCMEC) is the nation's resource center for child protection, with a 24-hour hotline, 1-800-THE-LOST: *www.ncmec.org/*.

Security awareness for Ma, Pa and the corporate clueless

A great resource for keeping your kids safe (Internet wise anyway) is the truly timeless and highly recommended book *Internet and Computer Ethics for Kids (and Their Parents and Teachers Who Haven't Got a Clue)* written by Winn Schwartau and illustrated by DL Busch. The book is available at: *www.thesecurityawarenesscompany.com/Ethics.html*.

Winn's website and efforts are highly regarded: *www.thesecurityawarenesscompany.com*.

PART 3: MAKING A DIFFERENCE

CHAPTER 15: LEARN FROM THE PAST AND "THINK"

Setting a goal is not the main thing. It is deciding how you will go about achieving it and staying with that plan.

Tom Landry

Nobody's perfect

While I never met W. Edwards Deming in person, this quote continues to inspire me:

You have heard the words; you must find the way. It will never be perfect. Perfection is not for this world; it is for some other world. I hope what you have heard here today will haunt you the rest of your life. I have done my best.

Continuous improvement really is a life-long journey: *http://blogs.itworldcanada.com/security/2009/01/23/dan-swanson-nobodys-perfect/*.

On quality management, Dr Deming, and candles: the last graduate student remembers her mentor

Lisa D McNary begins her article on Dr Deming with the following quote:

It's rather pleasant the way the human mind slips backwards and forwards through the years. Looking back through the years can be rather like walking down a corridor holding a candle. Incidents and places completely forgotten appear out of the blackness and, one by one, are lit as you pass. (Jean Hersey, *The Shape of a Year,* Charles Scribner & Sons, 1967)
www.spcpress.com/pdf/McNary.pdf

The goal: a process of ongoing improvement

Eli Goldratt (Eliyahu M Goldratt) is an educator, author, scientist, philosopher and business leader. However, he is, first and foremost, a thinker who provokes others to think. Often characterized as unconventional, stimulating, and "a slayer of sacred cows," Dr Goldratt exhorts his audience to examine and reassess their business practices with a fresh, new vision.

He is the author of *The Goal*, an underground best seller that utilizes a non-traditional approach to convey important business information – it is a business textbook written in novel form, disguised as a love story. The ideas illustrated in *The Goal* underscore Dr Goldratt's Theory of Constraints, an overall framework for helping businesses determine:

- what to change – not everything is broken
- what to change to – what are the simple, practical solutions
- how to cause the change – overcoming the inherent resistance to change.

www.eliyahugoldratt.com/

Crucial conversations: tools for talking when stakes are high

When stakes are high, opinions vary, and emotions run strong, you have three choices: avoid a crucial conversation and suffer the consequences; handle the conversation badly and suffer the consequences; or read *Crucial Conversations* and discover how to communicate best when it matters most. *Crucial Conversations* by Kerry Patterson, Joseph Grenny, Al Switzler and Ron McMillan (2002) gives you the tools you need to step up to life's most difficult and important conversations, say what's on your mind, and achieve the positive resolutions you want: *www.vitalsmarts.com/crucialconversations_book.aspx*.

Crucial confrontation: tools for resolving broken promises, violated expectations and bad behavior

Is accountability rock solid in your work culture? When co-workers make promises do you sigh in relief, or do you start biting your nails? Do you make plans, set goals, give assignments, and hope that maybe people will deliver?

With crucial confrontation skills you'll be able to:

- deal with violated expectations early, before they escalate into entrenched and chronic problems
- discuss disappointments without encountering defensiveness, resentment or even sabotage
- eliminate resistance by employing natural and enduring motivators
- hold everyone accountable to the same standards
- discuss challenges in a way that yields creative and eagerly supported solutions
- solve accountability problems without damaging the relationship: *www.vitalsmarts.com/crucialconfrontations_book.aspx*.

APPENDIX A: AN *EDPACS* ARTICLE

I have the pleasure of being the managing editor for the *EDPACS* publication. This monthly newsletter has covered audit, control and security topics for more than 40 years. Included here is one of my favorite *EDPACS* articles.

The state of IT auditing in 2007

Available at: *www.informaworld.com/smpp/title~content=g 781166228~db=all.*

Introduction

IT auditing has of course evolved as a specialism within audit, developing in importance alongside the growth of IT. Traditional audit aims and values (e.g. independent skilled assessment of risks and controls) apply equally to all auditors, and many of the skills and competencies are common. In fact, some of the specialist considerations of auditing computer systems are rapidly becoming mainstream because IT is an ubiquitous part of most audits, but we are getting ahead of ourselves. We will start this article by examining the historical and current factors influencing and driving the profession, characterize modern day IT auditors, explore their methods, tools, and techniques, and end by gazing into the crystal ball at the future directions of IT audit (*see Figure 1*).

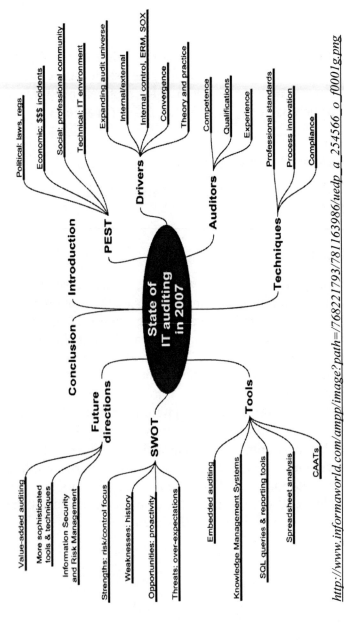

Figure 1: The state of IT auditing in 2007

http://www.informaworld.com/ampp/image?path=/768221793/781163986/uedp_a_254566_o_f0001g.png

PEST (environmental factors) analysis on IT audit

A common way to examine the influence of environmental factors on a subject area is to characterize the main political, economic/financial, social/sociological, and technical aspects, *see Table 1.*

Drivers and influences on the profession

Is your audit program focused on the right things, namely today's issues plus tomorrow's emerging threats? This is a significant question in the field of IT audit as things are moving ahead constantly in terms of technical advances in IT, changes in the way organizations are using IT, and improvements in IT audit capabilities. In this section, we will consider the factors that led us to where we are now, and continue changing the profession.

The expanding audit universe

In years gone by, auditors in the main were qualified accountants employed to give a second opinion on the integrity (quality, completeness, accuracy) of a company's accounts. The scope of audit was, therefore, very much based around the organization's finances – its accounting processes and standards, tax and latterly its accounting systems (general ledger, procurement, and sales systems). Audit's primary role was to give assurance to the stakeholders and authorities.

Table 1 *PEST Analysis*

Political	Economic
Although accounting laws have mandated audits of corporate finances by independent, qualified auditors for many years, we are gradually witnessing the introduction of laws and regulations requiring auditors to review computer systems, information processing, and other aspects such as corporate governance, health and safety, and so on. Professional standards are being documented and recommended for computer and other auditors by ISACA, IIA, AICPA, and similar organizations.	As the development and implementation of IT has progressed incessantly since the 1940/50s, information processing has become absolutely essential to most modern organizations, hence risks to information assets are more important than ever. Stakeholders and managers are looking to assess and manage their information risks and so are turning to specialist IT auditors for their independent, competent assessment of IT-related risks.

Social	Technical
There are many professional groups of IT auditors, collectively comprising a relatively supportive and close-knit community within the wider worlds of audit, risk/security management, and governance. "Bridging" or interpreting between the IT and business worlds has been an important role for IT auditors, given the number of business people with limited IT expertise and *vice versa*. Thankfully, this is becoming less of an issue as IT knowledge spreads into the wider business and IT people are increasingly taking business/management qualifications.	The advance of IT and telecommunications technologies creates a never-ending stream of issues of concern to IT auditors, while at the same time it is a source of new tools and techniques to do our jobs more effectively. The Internet is a good example: eBusiness and Internet connectivity substantially changes the organization's information security challenges, and provides IT auditors with access to a global knowledge base on auditing, technology, risk, control, security, governance, and every other topic imaginable.

As with the remainder of this article, the PEST analysis picks out aspects of and opinions on IT audit that the author feels are relevant and worth emphasizing.

Table 1: PEST analysis

To a large extent, this is still true of external audit although today's internal audit function typically has a broader remit, including other forms of audit (e.g. compliance against legal/regulatory obligations and internal company policies on aspects such as health and safety, environmental protection, and quality assurance) and internal management consultancy.

Many of the risks considered in a typical audit plan these days involve IT systems because accounting and other vital processes have been extensively computerized. At the same time as organizations have grown dependent on IT, we have seen a gradual increase in the level of information security threats and vulnerabilities. Relatively few audits (or auditors, for that matter!) can afford to ignore the computer systems and data networks supporting the business processes under review.

The evolving relationship between internal and external audit

External auditors are normally employed on behalf of shareholders and other owners to examine and provide a formal opinion on the organization's annual financial accounts (i.e. that they give a true and fair view, and are in line with the requirements of applicable laws and accounting practices). IT auditors working for an external audit company are primarily concerned with integrity of the client's core financial data and accounting systems, with a lower level of interest in the related/supporting systems and controls as a rule.

Internal auditors, by contrast, are employed by the organization's management to examine and comment on the organization's control systems and processes on an ongoing basis. They have no statutory authority so their work depends on management's direction coupled with generally accepted professional audit practices. Their remit usually extends well beyond the core financial processes, encompassing broader corporate governance and management control issues, for instance.

Internal and external auditors have a common interest in the financial systems plus the supporting systems and related controls. Whereas all IT auditors will probably review system security on the core financial systems, other IT systems and general information security controls are perhaps more likely to be reviewed by internal than external IT auditors, especially where the internal IT auditors are both competent and effective. External audit's perception of their internal audit colleagues influences the amount of confidence they can place in their work and hence the IT systems – in other words, external auditors normally review the work of internal auditors (thus partially answering the common question: "Who audits the auditors?"). They may go so far as to influence the annual internal audit plans, request special investigations, and so on.

In return, savvy internal audit functions have been known to turn the relationship with the external auditors to their advantage on occasions, for example directing the external auditors to scrutinize teams, IT systems, processes, and so on that have proven unduly resistant to internal audit. Managers who resent the involvement of internal auditors, frustrating audit work and ignoring audit recommendations, for example, may therefore find greater interest in their departments from the external auditors.

Appendix A: An EDPACS Article

Internal control, governance and compliance

The recent upsurge of interest in "GRC" (governance, risk and compliance or control) is a natural extension of the enormous amount of work in relation to the Sarbanes-Oxley Act (SOX), although the terms have been in use for decades. SOX compliance has been a massive issue for organizations listed on the US stock exchanges, including many based outside the US but with operations there. Prior to SOX, the governance movement started with a series of attempts at self regulation as far back as 1992 – Cadbury, the Combined Code, and COSO – but the WorldCom and Enron scandals triggered a heavy-handed regulatory response that few have escaped. Section 404 of SOX may once have seemed a relatively innocuous reference to the need for assurance on the integrity of financial systems, but has led to widespread review, documentation and dare-we-say improvement of information systems and networking controls.

COSO's Enterprise Risk Management (ERM) framework acknowledges the interaction between IT and other sources of risk. More people than ever before are asking about IT or information security risk-assessment techniques to direct the design and application of suitable IT controls. IT auditors are well positioned to provide objective advice to management on the suitability and likely effectiveness of proposed controls, particularly in situations where "technical solutions" neglect human factors such as policies and procedures.

Today, post-SOX, we are witnessing the increasing impact of other laws, professional standards, and industry regulations on IT audit. The ISO/IEC 27001 and 27002 information security standards, for instance, are entering an exponential growth phase and provide a convenient structured framework for IT auditors to review general security controls.

The IT Compliance Institute's Unified Compliance Project seeks to address the ever-increasing range of laws and regulations pertaining to IT governance, risk and security. The idea essentially is to identify common control requirements such that organizations can satisfy multiple objectives with fewer controls. This approach resembles the concept of the "security baseline"; in other words having a reasonably comprehensive set of controls implemented consistently by default, and additional controls individually specified and implemented as necessary to satisfy specific supra-baseline requirements (i.e. where the risks justify the additional investment). There are several benefits to IT auditors in such an approach, example:

- The organization needs to define its baseline, normally by preparing and mandating baseline security policies, standards, and guidelines. If well written, these leave little wiggle-room and make good specifications for compliance audits. Standards such as ISO27002 are useful as benchmarks for assessing the baselines.
- Implementation of the mandated baseline controls can be audited as a whole to confirm that there is a secure basis for the organization's IT infrastructure.
- Supra-baseline controls are supposed to be based on risk analysis and conscious architecture/design decisions, in which case there should be good evidence for the auditors to review in relation to identified high-risk aspects.

Appendix A: An EDPACS Article

Alignment of IT with the business

Continuing alignment of IT with business processes, leading in many cases to tight integration typical of eBusiness, makes the distinction increasingly irrelevant – IT is the business (and not just for computer manufacturers!). In the early days of IT, it was often seen as an ancillary/business support function and was typically managed by Finance Department, not least because of the high cost of early IT investments. Over the past decade, IT has become a department in its own right and now has something of a split personality: part support function, part driver of business innovation.

The economics of IT have evolved substantially over the same period. As hardware and software costs have plummeted, networked PCs, workgroup computers, and generic commercial software has overtaken expensive mainframe applications, point-to-point connections, and bespoke solutions in many areas. The commercial focus has moved from initial procurement toward whole lifecycle value management. Mainframes are very much alive, serving enterprise-wide applications and massive databases, while all manner of personal and embedded computer devices are all the rage. For the IT auditor, it is a personal and professional challenge to stay current with the technology explosion, and to remain in touch with business and strategic changes in relation to the use of IT.

Convergence of IT audit with information security, physical security, risk management and compliance

Another pressure on the profession is the alleged convergence of related specialist areas – I say alleged because although there is common ground, true multifunctional experts are still quite rare. For me, the original core values of audit inevitably set IT auditors apart from others: specifically, the objectivity that stems from audit's independence from routine operations and management. On the other hand, today's IT auditors need a working knowledge of many different areas in order to review and comment sensibly on them. The personal development opportunities that arise are a major attraction for many of us.

Theory and practice

Yogi Berra said: "In theory, there is no difference between theory and practice. In practice, there is." Creative auditors see audit methods and tools as a workman's tools – not boundaries on what they do, and by pushing the boundaries they expand the field for others. Academic contributions to the audit, risk, security and control areas are tempered by pragmatic developments and 'shortcuts' discovered by practitioners, and *vice versa*. In other words, tension between theoreticians and practitioners is a healthy sign of a developing profession. Take "Benford's law," for example, which arose from observations of number distributions plus number theory, and has practical application in searching for possible data manipulation and fraud. Benford's law alone is not sufficient to detect all frauds, merely a certain type involving specific number distributions. Well-rounded IT auditors should know when to apply Benford's law when reviewing a data set for anomalies, but they will also examine many other aspects for fraud opportunities and evidence.

Appendix A: An EDPACS Article

Characteristics of today's IT auditor

IT auditor competences and personality traits

There are two main career paths leading to IT audit: firstly, from technology (often information security, IT operations, IT project management, systems development, or business analysis), and alternatively from accountancy (general or financial audit, financial or management accounting). Other accepted/common entry routes include:

- Accountancy.
- Other types of auditing (e.g. financial audit, quality audit, health and safety audit and legal, regulatory or other compliance work [auditors who have been auditing business processes for years almost certainly have some familiarity with IT audit techniques, and may progress into the specialism. In general, though, successful IT auditors have a deep fascination with technology for technology's sake. They enjoy the special challenges that IT auditing presents.])
- IT and/or management consultancy.
- Risk management, especially IT risk management.
- "Security" as in the police and military/government intelligence.
- Other technical management roles and sometimes even non-technical managers (who rely heavily on the support of technologically competent IT auditors in their team).
- University, college, or school-leavers (who are often well qualified but lack the practical experience and so start as juniors).

Information security is arguably the most closely allied field to IT audit because it also encompasses the concepts of risk and control in relation to computer and telecommunications systems, and senior information security staff normally have reasonably good working relationships with both IT and "the business" (outside of IT).

In just the same way that tax auditors get deep into their field, way beyond the level that most of us would even contemplate, so do IT auditors. Immersion in IT-related risks, security controls and governance issues leads to competence, credibility and strengths borne of knowledge and familiarity with complex concepts that often baffle others. Coupled with audit's independence and structured audit methods, noted earlier, plus the strength of character to stand up for what's right, competent IT auditors bring unique skills and advantages to the organizations they serve.

Taking the wider view, another extremely important characteristic of competent auditors, including IT auditors, is their personal trustworthiness and integrity. IT auditors are likely to gain extensive access to systems and data in the course of their work, and typically possess the knowledge and skills to compromise security controls if they so choose – all they lack is the motivation. This is essentially the same issue as with all holders of privileged user IDs and other highly trusted roles within the organization. No amount of background checking, personality/psychometric tests, and so on, can prove that an individual is absolutely honest and true, but diligent IT auditors take pains to avoid any conflicts of interest or doubts about what they are doing, such as insisting on read-only access to systems being audited and logging their own activities.

Appendix A: An EDPACS Article

Aside from the formal qualifications, practical on-the-job experience is a major advantage, particularly for the softer skills such as interviewing techniques and establishing rapport, especially with evasive or nervous auditees. Perhaps the most important benefit of audit experience is a thorough understanding of risk and control concepts. Auditors specialize in advising management on the need for controls to address the risks that they observe and/or surmise. IT auditors need to:

- identify actual and potential risks to the business associated with computer systems, networks, IT installations, applications, development projects, and so on
- observe and review technical, physical, and procedural controls in operation
- assess whether the level of risk is reasonable or whether control improvements are required
- justify and recommend more-or-less specific control improvements, persuading management to commit to resourcing and making the changes within a sensible timeframe (remembering that it's management's job to make the decisions, not theirs).

IT auditors' core expertise is naturally focused on ICT (information and communications technologies), but their expertise in risk and control concepts has broader application. Reviewing and discussing ICT risks and controls in relation to the organizational environment as a whole is a powerful technique for influencing management. This implies a further competence at bridging between the worlds of technology and business. A reasonable understanding of, and respect for, change management concepts and business management in general, are likely to make the IT auditor more effective overall.

IT auditors, like all auditors, need to be well aware of "corporate politics" to deal efficiently with the strong personalities characteristic of most senior managers. At times, they certainly need thick skins! Other advantageous personality characteristics include: inquisitiveness, objectivity or independence of thought, assertiveness, analytical abilities (cognitive abilities, intelligence), proactivity and diligence, pragmatism and communications skills (report writing, presenting, discussing and negotiating).

IT audit qualifications

Professional qualifications bring two key benefits: firstly, students study toward the certifications and, therefore, become better educated, and secondly, they demonstrate achievement of a certain level of competence. Audit-related qualifications are obviously central to any IT auditor's employment prospects but in addition many other qualifications are potentially applicable and relevant to IT auditors. The range has been expanding steadily since the 1980s to include the following (and more):

- ABCP, CBCP, & MBCP (Associate, Certified & Master Business Continuity Professional certifications) from DRII, the Disaster Recovery Institute International
- BSc, MSc, PhD, and similar academic qualifications in IT auditing, information security, risk management, and related topics
- CCE (Certified Computer Examiner) from the International Society of Forensic Computer Examiners

- CCO (Certified Confidentiality Officer) from BECCA, the Business Espionage, Controls and Countermeasures Association
- CEH (Certified Ethical Hacker), CHFI (Computer Hacking Forensic Investigator), LPT (Licensed Penetration Tester), and ECSA (EC-Council Certified Security Analyst) from the International Council of E-Commerce Consultants
- Certificate in Information Security Management Principles from BCS, the British Computer Society
- CFE (Certified Fraud Examiner) from ACFE, the Association of Certified Fraud Examiners
- CISA (Certified Information Systems Auditor) from ISACA
- CISM (Certified Information Security Manager) from ISACA
- general IT (not audit/security specific) qualifications (especially those with significant information security, risk, and control content), (non-IT) audit qualifications, management, and accountancy qualifications
- GIAC (Global Information Assurance Certification) by SANS
- ISSPCS (International Systems Security Professional Certification Scheme) from the International Systems Security Engineering Association (ISSEA)
- language skills – a strong command of English (or your own native tongue) and the ability to write in a formal, objective yet persuasive style is essential
- MCSE:security and MCSA:security (Microsoft Certified Systems Engineer and Administrator certifications with security specialism) from Microsoft
- other specialist qualifications such as tax, law, HR, quality, safety, and so on

- PCI & CPP (Professional Certified Investigator and Certified Protection Professional) from ASIS International
- CIP (Professional in Critical Infrastructure Protection) from the Critical Infrastructure Institute
- Security+ from CompTIA, the Computing Technology Industry Association
- SSCP (Systems Security Certified Practitioner) and CISSP (Certified Information Systems Security Professional) from (ISC), plus specializations such as ISSAP, ISSEP, and ISSMP (Information Systems Security Architecture/Engineering/Management Professional, respectively)
- Various vendor-specific security and related qualifications, particularly those from suppliers of security products such as Check Point, Cisco, Guidance Software, and TruSecure.

Of the qualifications listed here, CISA is widely recognized as the primary qualification for IT auditors with the remainder being of value when auditing particular IT risks and controls. More than 50,000 IT auditors have been CISA-certified since 1978. The CISA examination is conducted by ISACA in nearly 100 countries and 11 languages.

Experience

Depending on the seniority of the post and the level of support available (e.g. whether the individual IT auditor will work alone or as part of a team), the amount of professional experience needed for a job in IT audit varies. At the risk of over-generalizing, an individual's success usually correlates with the breadth and depth of their business and IT experience prior to becoming an IT auditor, coupled with their willingness to learn more on the job.

Once signed-up as a IT auditor, genuine personal and professional development is far more than simply a matter of gathering the requisite number of "CPEs" (Continuous Professional Education credits) to renew qualifications such as CISA, CISM, and CISSP. The best IT auditors have an incessant thirst for knowledge based on a deep fascination with technology, audit, and related aspects.

On the other hand, success is not necessarily related to the IT auditor's age. There is even a danger that although "grey beards" may have an immense depth of experience, they may be too set in their ways to appreciate some of the new risks and opportunities facing them. "Life experience" is no bad thing though, especially when it brings wisdom and the natural ability to empathize with auditees.

IT audit techniques, methods, and tools

Techniques and methods

First, let's take a look at the range of IT-related audit work that IT auditors typically undertake in the course of their careers:

- **Operational computer system/network audits**: review the information security and other controls within and surrounding operational computer systems and networks.
- **IT installation audits**: review the computer building, suite, room, or cupboard, including aspects such as physical security, environmental controls, computer and network operations processes and management systems and, of course, the IT equipment itself.

- **Developing systems audits**: typically cover either or both of two aspects: (1) project/program management controls; and (2) the implementation of appropriate information security controls within and supporting the developed system.
- **IT governance, management and strategic audits**: review the organization, structure, strategy, work planning, resource planning, budgeting, cost controls, and so on, and, where applicable, relationships with outsourced IT providers. Also review IT strategies, visions, and plans, including their relationship to other strategies, visions, and plans.
- **IT process audits**: review processes within IT such as application development, testing, implementation, operations, maintenance, housekeeping (backups, preventive maintenance, etc.), support, incident handling.
- **Change management audits**: review the planning and control of changes to systems, networks, applications, processes, facilities, and so on, including configuration management and controls over the promotion of code from development through testing to production.
- **Information security and control audits**: review technical, procedural and other controls protecting the confidentiality, integrity and availability of systems and data.
- **IT compliance audits**: review compliance with external requirements (i.e. IT-related laws and regulations such as SOX, PCI, software copyright and personal data/privacy) and internal/corporate requirements (IT/information security policies, standards, procedures and guidelines).

- **Benchmarking:** comparing the IT performance, efficiency, and/or capabilities of an organization to other similar organizations, or comparing business units within a large organization, or measuring against generally accepted standards.

- **Contingency planning:** review business continuity and IT disaster recovery plans and the associated processes (e.g. tests and exercises).

- **Special investigations:** contingency and un-pre-planned work such as investigating suspected frauds or information security breaches, performing due diligence review of IT assets for mergers and acquisitions, and investigating incident reports from whistle-blowers.

- **Other:** IT auditors often work alongside financial, operational, and other non-IT auditors, supplementing the team with expertise on the IT systems aspects. They may contribute to risk assessment workshops and at times may offer IT consultancy advice or mentoring to risk, security and compliance professionals, including those within the audit team.

IT audits follow the same process as all audits, namely:

- **Audit schedule or plan** – management decides which parts of the audit universe to audit and when. The output of the planning process is typically an outline audit scope, a timescale, and resource allocation for each audit.

- **Scoping and pre-audit survey** – the auditors determine the main area/s of focus and any areas that are explicitly out-of-scope, based normally on some form of risk-based assessment. Information sources at this stage include background reading and Web browsing, previous audit reports, and sometimes, subjective impressions that deserve further investigation.

- **Planning and preparation** – during which the scope is broken down into greater levels of detail, usually involving the generation of an audit workplan, checklist, or risk-control-matrix.

- **Fieldwork** – gathering evidence by interviewing staff and managers, reviewing documents, printouts and data, observing processes, and so on. This step may include the use of Computer Aided Audit Techniques (CAATs) – see the section on IT audit tools for more.

- **Analysis of the evidence gathered earlier** – the PEST and SWOT tables in this article are examples of the kinds of analytical techniques that may be used. Knowledgebase and audit-decision support tools may help.

- **Reporting** – is the primary focus of the audit process and a great deal of attention is paid to it by both auditors and auditees. It is a fairly complex sub-process all by itself. See more information later.

- **Closure** – in addition to completing and literally shutting the audit files, closure involves preparing notes for future audits, updating risk models, and, in some organizations, following up with management to confirm that the actions they agreed on are completed. Neither the best nor the worst organizations do audit follow-ups, in both cases because there is literally no point. Most organizations however do need to "close the loop."

Reporting of IT audits is just as involved as reporting any other audit, albeit often with the added complication of having to explain complex technical issues to a varied audience. The previously mentioned IT auditors' skills at bridging IT and business worlds, formal writing and presentation, and sensitivity to corporate politics, come into their own in this phase. In addition, the strengths of the audit method (i.e. systematic assessment of risks followed by painstaking collection and analysis of reliable supporting evidence) normally provides the basis for compelling reports. Creative thinking and brainstorming techniques can help generate effective audit recommendations without overly constraining auditees (it is often worthwhile involving auditees in the brainstorming process). Although the internal quality assurance and interaction with senior auditees inevitably slow the process to a crawl, this is an expected part of the wider change process – do not forget that the key purpose of audit is to improve the organization, changing it for the better, not just to issue smart reports.

On that last point, IT auditors at times aim to reinforce the existing controls infrastructure (for instance, through IT policy compliance audits) and sometimes seek further development of the controls infrastructure (e.g. changing systems and processes to introduce new security controls). Innovation applies to both in the sense of helping the organization find creative means to navigate its way past barriers.

IT audit tools

COBIT and Val IT

COBIT has changed significantly since originally being developed by ISACA and released as "Control Objectives for Information and related Technologies." I personally recall exploring COBIT about a decade ago but finding it tricky to apply in practice. It was transferred to the IT Governance Institute (ITGI) and was recently revised to version 4.1. COBIT focuses primarily on the governance and management processes within IT. As a method, it is well suited to a painstaking, structured analysis of the control of IT system and process inputs, transformations, and outputs.

Val IT, based on COBIT (version 2.0 released in 2008), is a framework and best practice guidance from ITGI focusing on enterprise governance of IT for business benefit. It addresses the governance process and the management processes for selecting a portfolio of investments and then managing those programs to create for the organization.

CAATs (Computer Aided Audit Tools)

CAATs are tools or utilities that help auditors select, analyze and report audit findings. Specialized CAAT programs such as ACL (Audit Control Language) and IDEA (Interactive Data Extraction and Analysis) provide functions plus libraries of prewritten queries that help sample and examine data sets. Utilities such as WizRule help auditors explore complex data sets, spreadsheets, and other IT applications.

Here are some simple examples of the kinds of issues a CAAT might address:

- What were the top 10% of transactions by value last March?
- How many changes were made to the customer details file during the previous year?
- Are there any out-of-range/unusual data values or suspicious data patterns in column 4?
- Are any of our suppliers also employees?

CAATs are a great help when asking complex audit questions or reviewing large data sets. Big CAAT queries can take hours to run, but the utility of the output is proportional to the quality of the question asked, rather than the time taken *per se*. It still takes expertise/skill and judgment on the part of the auditor to interpret the results sensibly and develop worthwhile recommendations.

Audit automation and workflow tools

All auditors use computers (especially mobile equipment such as laptops, PDAs and mobile phones) as work tools. Whereas many audit functions use standard office software to plan and document their work, some rely on audit automation tools such as TeamMate to support the process. The structured nature of most audits lends itself to a degree of automation ranging from simple templates for the standard forms and reports to process flow, decision support and knowledge management tools. Such tools are designed for all auditors, although because of their IT expertise, IT auditors quite often get more involved in selecting, implementing and maintaining the tools on behalf of their colleagues.

Other IT audit tools

Various IT development, operations and information security applications (such as software-development workflow programs, change/configuration management software, intrusion detection/prevention systems, application security, and penetration testing tools) may help IT auditors find and evaluate control weaknesses. Vulnerability assessment tools such as the Center for

Internet Security's system security benchmarks, NIST's security configuration checklists and Microsoft Baseline Security Advisor automate tedious configuration checks to search for common security weaknesses in Windows, UNIX, and other platforms plus major applications, such as SAP. Again, it takes expertise/skill and judgment to interpret the results sensibly.

Risk management methods and tools

IT auditors typically use methods and tools such as the following to support risk analyses, and so on:

- AS/NZS 4360: a well-respected risk management standard and guideline.
- Citicus ONE: a commercial software product based on the FIRM information security risk analysis method originally developed by the Information Security Forum.
- CRAMM: originally developed for UK government use as "CCTA Risk Assessment and Management Methodology."
- Mehari: a French risk analysis and management method.
- NIST SP 800-30: *Risk Management Guide for Information Technology Systems.*
- OCTAVE "Operationally Critical Threat, Asset, and Vulnerability Evaluation": CERT's risk-based strategic assessment and planning technique for security.
- Proteus Enterprise: a security risk management support tool.

Appendix A: An EDPACS Article

Audit functions built in to systems

Finally, in this section, we must mention the functions and facilities built in to well-designed computer systems to make the auditors' job easier. Examples include audit trails recording important user and administrator activities, system security logs, exception reporting subsystems, and all manner of integrity or other self-checks. These span the gap between standalone audit tools and miscellaneous system controls required by the business users – they typically both support routine operations and management, as well as audits. IT auditors should get involved in specifying requirements for audit functions and facilities for the auditors, and often need to prompt business managers to specify their routine requirements also.

SWOT analysis on IT audit

Table 2 summarizes some of the key strengths, weaknesses, opportunities and threats to the IT audit profession. The left-hand side of the table is generally positive, whereas the right-hand side is more negative. The top half of the table focuses on the past and present, whereas the bottom projects forward in time.

Table 2 SWOT Analysis

Strengths	Weaknesses
IT/information risk, control/security, and governance focused specialism. Provides independent, objective assessment. Provides assurance to stakeholders. Applies structured methods systematically and rigorously. Increasingly viewed as a true profession.	Audit is viewed historically as an accounting review function, a rather cynical and negative one at that—the business benefits of auditing are seldom promoted or understood except perhaps at executive board level. IT auditors who focus too deeply on the technology may miss the wider organizational context and human issues, hence neglecting important business risks.
Opportunities	**Threats**
Collaboration with non-IT auditors and other business people. Strong IT audit tools, techniques, and methods (more later). Proactive auditing (e.g., tracking software development projects from cradle to grave). Innovative change catalyst. Global cross-fertilization of best IT and business practices.	Over-commitment—IT is everywhere. Unreasonable expectations due to complexities both within the technology and in the way it is used and abused. Being put into the "compliance" box (e.g., the function is to assess compliance with SOX, not to stimulate/promote added value). Dissolution of IT audit as a discrete specialism because virtually all auditors need IT audit skills.

Table 2: SWOT analysis

Appendix A: An EDPACS Article

Future directions for the profession

I would like to predict some of the ways in which I see IT auditing changing over the next decade or so to conclude this article. Although I claim no special powers and offer no guarantees, I simply hope that the following notes will encourage you to seek out opportunities to improve the profession.

Technology advancements

Very few organizations indeed can claim to have been entirely unaffected by the Internet. The Internet has dominated IT developments for more than a decade and seems likely to continue in this vein for the foreseeable future. For auditors, the Web obviously gives ready access to global communities of peers and vast amounts of information (although unfortunately not equally valuable). Developments such as Voice over IP (VoIP), Software as a Service (SaaS – formerly known as Application Service Provider, ASP) and Web 2.0 present new challenges for auditors (and perhaps even business opportunities for entrepreneurial auditors?). Speaking generically, technology advancements change the risk landscape. Auditors need to recognize and respond appropriately to such changes, ideally at the earliest stages of application by their organizations.

Adding value to the organization through IT audit

All auditors, and indeed all employees and consultants, claim to add value to their employers and client organizations. The particular value that IT auditors bring is in identifying improvement opportunities and promoting beneficial changes in the way IT is used and controlled. It is no longer enough for the auditors simply to point out that a certain computer system has weak user authentication controls that should be strengthened as a matter of good practice: business managers increasingly expect to evaluate the costs and benefits of making such changes, with an emphasis on achieving net value. IT auditors who appreciate the need to justify the costs relating to their recommendations by estimating the business benefits, and perhaps to assess related issues such as strategic fit, stand to make better, more convincing recommendations. This implies that IT auditors should have business as well as technology skills and training. The auditors should anticipate and respond appropriately to robust challenges on the assumptions and projections underlying their value forecasts, from managers who (perhaps through SOX) appreciate the difficulties inherent in predicting the future. On the other hand, rigorous audit methods coupled with skills and qualifications puts experienced IT auditors in a relatively strong position. Overcoming the organization's natural inertia and resistance to change is valuable in itself.

Evaluating people, processes and technology

IT auditors work at the intersection between the IT systems and the people who specify, develop, implement, use, manage and maintain them, and thus need to be competent and comfortable with both aspects. When evaluating technical system vulnerabilities, for instance, the auditor clearly needs a strong understanding of the technology in order to identify and characterize genuine technical issues. Further, it is entirely reasonable for the auditor to explore the reasons why known vulnerabilities were not identified and resolved (e.g. by patching) by the systems managers and others – perhaps even to challenge the original technical architects, developers, testers and administrators of the faulty system. There are many other types of IT audit assignment, as noted earlier, all of which involve reviewing both technologies and humans to varying extents. IT auditors therefore need to work on their people as well as technical skills, quite a challenge for the "geek" personality types so often attracted to careers in IT. Merely appreciating that there are different personality types is a good start!

Although most IT auditors are generalists, competent and able to audit practically any IT system or situation, there are early signs of specialization within IT audit. As IT audit teams have grown consistently beyond the typical starting point of just one person, so the potential arises for individuals within the team to specialize in, say, mainframe or network auditing. There are already specialisms in areas of information security, such as security architecture and cryptography, with the associated education and certification schemes starting to gain recognition. It seems likely that IT audit specialisms will emerge over the next decade or two.

Cooperation between auditors and blurring the lines between them (integrated audit)

Until the end of the twentieth century, deciding whether to audit "around" or "through" the computer systems was an important choice in the planning stage of many audits. Due to their limited familiarity with IT, many non-IT auditors (and indeed many non-IT business people) treated computer systems as "black boxes." Non-IT auditors, therefore, restricted their work to the surrounding business processes and artefacts, in some cases manually re-calculating figures to confirm that the IT systems were calculating correctly. IT auditors, in contrast, were seen as the experts in auditing computers and restricted their work accordingly, largely ignoring the business processes. Blurring the lines was the idea of "integrated auditing" that emerged in the 1990s: all auditors need a reasonable understanding of both the technology and the business.

Some predict that the days of "IT audit" are numbered, given that so much audit work necessarily involves using and reviewing the computer systems and data that drive modern business. Although personally I agree that all auditors need to appreciate the value of and risks inherent in information systems, I suspect that the depth of technical knowledge required to understand the limitations of systems security (for example) is probably beyond both the capabilities and interests of most non-IT auditors. In my experience, IT auditors complement their colleagues and *vice versa*. Similarly, I suspect that there will always be a demand for auditors who specialize in finance, tax, health and safety, environmental protection, fraud, law, and so on, supplementing the general knowledge of other auditors. It is no trivial matter to stay current with developments in any of these fields of knowledge.

That said, IT auditors frequently work alongside other auditors in mixed teams. Team working brings opportunities for bidirectional skills transfer, plus greater appreciation of the others' points of view. Furthermore, collaboration between internal and external IT auditors can create benefits for both. Moving forward, IT auditors who treat these touch points as challenges to "their" territory are likely to find themselves sidelined whereas those who embrace the changes will thrive on the development opportunities, becoming more rounded professionals and more effective to boot.

Maturity as a profession

ISACA traces its origins back to the EDP Auditors Association formed in 1969, which later became the Information Systems Audit and Control Association before finally dropping the long name in favor of the acronym. It has been guiding IT auditors for nearly four decades, introducing professional methods, standards, guidelines, and qualifications that are well respected by audit practitioners and others.

Throughout its history, ISACA has supported and represented its members, today more than 86,000 strong in over 160 countries. ISACA's Journal sits alongside *EDPACS* as a leading technical journal in the information control field. ISACA conferences and workshops attract large numbers of participants.

ISACA established the IT Governance Institute (ITGI) in 1998. ITGI undertakes research to help senior managers fulfill their IT governance responsibilities by using IT successfully to support the enterprise's mission and goals.

In 2005, a strategic partnership between ISACA, ISSA (the Information Systems Security Association with 13,000 members) and ASIS International (the American Society for Industrial Security with 35,000 members) was announced in response to the convergence pressures on IT audit, information security and physical security professionals. Unfortunately, there has not been much to show from the partnership to date, despite the potential for members sharing benefits and cross-skilling. It is difficult even to find mention of the partnership on the websites of the three partners. However, the convergence pressures are still there, although audit independence obviously limits the extent to which IT auditors can sensibly merge with their colleagues in information, physical security, or other fields.

IT audit is not terribly well understood except by those working within the profession. Auditing in general has negative connotations, not helped by the perception that audit implies "tick-and-bash" compliance reviews and grief. Despite this, there is a reasonable level of interest in joining the profession judging by the number of inquiries on the Institute of Internal Audit IT audit discussion board and comments on my computer audit FAQ, and the number of CISAs continues to grow. I would encourage all IT auditors to watch out for potential new recruits among the auditees and their work colleagues. Further, I feel it would be beneficial for ISACA and (ISC) to move beyond promoting their individual certifications toward jointly raising the profile and value of both IT audit and information security professions. There are interesting times ahead.

Conclusion

I have presented an overview of the origins and current state of IT audit, discussed some of the pressures on the profession today, and gazed into the future to predict changes barely started as yet. Along the way, I reviewed the range of methods, tools and techniques available to IT auditors, outlined their qualifications, skills, and competencies, and used two common audit techniques (PEST and SWOT) to analyze the internal and external influences. Stepping back a pace or two, I hope you can better appreciate the value that IT audit brings to the organization, maybe even enough to consider joining the profession.

Written by Gary Hinson and first published in *EDPACS.*[35]

---

[35] Published in 2007 (volume 36, issue 1). Please see the actual article for footnote references.

APPENDIX B: INTERNATIONAL STANDARDS FOR THE PROFESSIONAL PRACTICE OF INTERNAL AUDITING (STANDARDS)[36]

Attribute Standards

1000 – Purpose, Authority, and Responsibility

The purpose, authority, and responsibility of the internal audit activity must be formally defined in an internal audit charter, consistent with the Definition of Internal Auditing, the Code of Ethics, and the Standards. The chief audit executive must periodically review the internal audit charter and present it to senior management and the Board for approval.

Interpretation

The internal audit charter is a formal document that defines the internal audit activity's purpose, authority, and responsibility. The internal audit charter establishes the internal audit activity's position within the organization; authorizes access to records, personnel, and physical properties relevant to the performance of engagements; and defines the scope of internal audit activities. Final approval of the internal audit charter resides with the Board.

- 1000.A1 – The nature of assurance services provided to the organization must be defined in the internal audit charter. If assurances are to be provided to parties

---

[36] To obtain a copy of the entire set of internal audit standards go to:
http://www.theiia.org/guidance/standards-and-guidance/ippf/standards/.

269

outside the organization, the nature of these assurances must also be defined in the internal audit charter.

- 1000.C1 – The nature of consulting services must be defined in the internal audit charter.

Performance Standards

2000 – Managing the Internal Audit Activity

The chief audit executive must effectively manage the internal audit activity to ensure it adds value to the organization.

Interpretation:

The internal audit activity is effectively managed when:

- The results of the internal audit activity's work achieve the purpose and responsibility included in the internal audit charter;
- The internal audit activity conforms with the Definition of Internal Auditing and the Standards; and
- The individuals who are part of the internal audit activity demonstrate conformance with the Code of Ethics and the Standards.

APPENDIX C: GLOBAL TECHNOLOGY AUDIT GUIDES

Global Technology Audit Guides (GTAG®)

Prepared by the Institute of Internal Auditors (IIA), each Global Technology Audit Guide (GTAG) is written in straightforward business language to address a timely issue related to information technology (IT) management, control and security.

> The GTAG series serves as a ready resource for chief audit executives on different technology-associated risks and recommended practices:
> *http://www.theiia.org/guidance/standards-and-guidance/ippf/practice-guides/gtag/.*

Practice guides are restricted to IIA members only. Learn more about becoming a member at: *www.theiia.org/membership/why-join/.*

PG GTAG-15: Information Security Governance

PG GTAG-14: Auditing User-developed Applications

PG GTAG-13: Fraud Prevention and Detection in an Automated World

PG GTAG-12: Auditing IT Projects

PG GTAG-11: Developing the IT Audit Plan

PG GTAG-10: Business Continuity Management

PG GTAG-9: Identity and Access Management

Appendix C: Global Technology Audit Guides

PG GTAG-8: Auditing Application Controls

PG GTAG-7: Information Technology Outsourcing

PG GTAG-6: Managing and Auditing IT Vulnerabilities

PG GTAG-5: Managing and Auditing Privacy Risks

PG GTAG-4: Management of IT Auditing

PG GTAG-3: Continuous Auditing: Implications for Assurance, Monitoring, and Risk Assessment

PG GTAG-2: Change and Patch Management Controls: Critical for Organizational Success

PG GTAG-1: Information Technology Controls

APPENDIX D: A PRIMER ON CORPORATE DUTIES [37]

The information contained in this Appendix must not be relied upon as legal advice. We try to provide quality information, but cannot be responsible for the accuracy, completeness, or adequacy of the information contained herein as it applies to specific situations. As legal advice must be tailored to the specific circumstances of each case, and laws are constantly changing, nothing provided herein should be used as a substitute for the advice of competent legal counsel.

Introduction

In the simplest of terms, members of the Board have a fiduciary duty and obligation to serve the best interests of shareholders. That obligation may differ from state to state and due to stock exchange guidelines or special circumstances. Recent decisions make it clear that directors are responsible for keeping up with "best practices" in corporate governance and for compliance with laws and regulations. Concentrating on the adherence to principles of excellence in corporate governance will demonstrate the Board has fulfilled their fiduciary obligation in compliance

---

[37] This appendix, entitled 'Appendix E: A Primer on Corporate Duties' in the actual document, comprises generalizations of corporate duties and is provided to raise awareness of the numerous and complex issues involved in corporate governance. This primer is reprinted with permission and was originally published in the OCEG *Internal Audit Guide* (www.oceg.org).

with relevant laws and regulations. Officers and managers generally are not discussed in this Appendix.

The Audit Committee of the Board of Directors are further charged with adhering to all applicable accounting standards, accounting controls, audit practices and making use of the internal audit function. The Audit Committee must establish procedures relating to the receipt, retention, and action on complaints regarding accounting, internal accounting controls, external and internal auditing matters by employees and sometimes others. Because when employees are protected, and encouraged to come forward and truthfully report on believed violations without fear of dismissal or retaliation, including threatening, harassing, or discriminating against them; they will do exactly that.

The Federal Sentencing Guidelines may increase or decrease a corporation's or director's penalty based upon recklessness or precautions for the activities of corporations, but they do not create responsibility where the law does not otherwise impose it. Directors would be well served to review those Guidelines at least annually, and to review compliance programs frequently.

Evidence that a corporation has implemented an internal audit function along with evidence that the Board and the Audit Committee understand these responsibilities and those programs are being monitored for compliance with mandated governance and ethics issues, may mitigate corporate penalties or limit prosecutorial focus to culpable individuals, rather than the corporation.

Appendix D: A Primer on Corporate Duties

Duty of Care

Duty of Care applies to directors. Directors are expected to exercise ordinary care in the discharge of their duties. The duty of care requires directors to perform their responsibilities in an informed businesslike manner.

The MBCA[38] identifies the standards of conduct that are expected of directors as a duty to act: (i) in good faith; and (ii) in a manner he or she reasonably believes to be in the best interests of the corporation. In addition, when becoming informed in connection with their decision-making function or devoting attention to their oversight function, directors must exercise the care that a person in a like position would reasonably believe appropriate under similar circumstances.

The MBCA further describes a director's duties to include duty of care, duty of inquiry, duty of informed judgment, duty of attention, duty of loyalty, duty of fair dealing, and the fiduciary duties of directors. Not all of these duties have been recognized by the courts of Delaware, although some cases in other jurisdictions have gone further than Delaware. Directors are expected to devote adequate time and attention to the corporation as well as the skill and judgment reflected in reasoned business decisions. Diligence in the management and administration of the

---

[38] Legislation dealing with corporate duties is the jurisdiction of each individual state in the US. To aid in the uniformity of these laws, the Committee on Corporate Laws of the American Bar Association has drafted a Model Business Corporation Act ('MBCA'), which has been revised from time to time. While the MBCA has been adopt by most states, the various provisions of the MBCA have no legal force or effect until they are adopted by each states.

In Canada, depending on which act a corporation is formed under, corporate duties are governed either provincially, under a particular province's corporations act or federally, under the Canada Business Corporations Act ("CBCA").

corporation's affairs and in the use and preservation of its assets is expected. Directors are also expected to stay informed about the corporation's affairs. Concepts of director liability for losses and damages to the corporation have long been recognized. Questions of the degree to which care has been exercised are the subject of fact specific inquiry in each case.

To the extent that the directors have met their duties of care, they must also act within the scope of their authority and avoid breaching the terms of their corporate charter. Their liability will vary from state to state.

In Canada, the CBCA similarly imposes a duty of care upon directors:

> (i)   to act honestly, in good faith and in the best interest of the corporation; and

> (ii)   to exercise the care, diligence and skill of a reasonably prudent person

Duty of Loyalty

The essence of this fiduciary duty is the subordination of one's own interest to that of the corporation. Generally, directors should not appear on both sides of a transaction nor derive any personal benefit from it in the form of self dealing, which would differ from that enjoyed by the shareholders of the corporation.   The duty of loyalty imposes on such persons a duty to avoid (or at least clearly and unequivocally disclose) any conflicts of interest, elevate the interests of the corporation above their own individual gain, and not deprive the corporation of any advantage to which it is entitled.

However, both the MBCA and the CBCA provide instances in which such personal gain by directors may be acceptable. Generally, where a conflict of interest exists, the transaction may proceed if it has been fully disclosed and approved by "disinterested directors" or "Qualified Directors". However, as previously stated, each jurisdiction may have developed its own set of rules with respect to these types of transactions, and such transactions are usually determined on a case-by-case basis.

Determining Liability

Potential exposure to litigation can result from a failure to act in situations in which due attention would arguably have prevented a loss and this is not new. The standard of care already distinguishes negligent inaction from an erroneous decision and the standards for determining liability have not substantially changed, though the courts appear to be examining compliance more carefully. For example, the directors in the Disney compensation case were exonerated even though their procedures were not a model of conduct.

Sarbanes-Oxley did not change general fiduciary duties and it did not add explicit penalties for directors who fail to discharge their duties in these areas. Presumably, they are subject to the same penalties as always existed. But rather, it increased legal requirements in the financial and accounting area. SOX has increased the duties of directors (and especially audit committee members) to monitor accounting, accounting decisions and the relationship between the corporation and its auditors. Although a few cases, such as Adelphia, include allegations of the violation of the new certification requirements, the most notorious cases are being prosecuted under the existing law, not SOX.

Due to the novelty of the Sarbanes-Oxley Act and its Canadian equivalents, the full extent of directors' liabilities under these new statutes is yet to be determined.

Courts are now applying greater scrutiny to the actions of directors and officers of insolvent or nearly insolvent companies; evaluating the company's actions and their impact on the overall business enterprise, not merely shareholders. Actions by directors and officers and managers of these companies are coming under ever-increasing levels of review, and the courts may begin placing more stringent expectations on their performance of fiduciary obligations. See Effects of the Zone of Insolvency on Fiduciary Duties below.

Business Judgment Rule

The business judgment rule shields directors from liability for their errors or mistakes if they performed their duties in good faith and they did so in a manner that they reasonably believed to be in the best interests of the corporation. The rule prevents the use of hindsight to impose alternative decisions on the corporation. It expresses judicial reluctance to interfere in the internal affairs of a corporation and a desire not to substitute judicial and legal judgments for those of the directors. There is no concept of general care in acting as a director. The care applies to the gathering of information, etc., but not to the decisions.

Generally, the business judgment of directors has been deferred to if they have arrived at their decision in a conscientious and diligent manner. Such diligence may include investigating the full spectrum of the circumstances involved and the facts surrounding the subject matter before making their decisions. They may rely on information provided to them by officers and employees as well as outside professionals or committees if they reasonably believe these sources are reliable and competent.

Officers and managers generally are not discussed in this appendix. The rule generally is not applicable to officers because they do not exercise the general supervisory duties imposed on the Board and shareholders generally do not have direct recourse against officers.

In recent years, questions about the nature of these duties and obligations have centered upon a review of past patterns of conduct in each particular case. Courts have also refused to use the business judgment rule to protect directors when there was no evidence of an exercise of judgment. These developments place an increased emphasis on documenting decisions, discussions and voting prior to its approval of company transactions.

Effects of the Zone of Insolvency on Fiduciary Duties

Most courts have determined that directors and officers of solvent corporations do not owe fiduciary duties to creditors. It has become almost hornbook law that when a corporation enters the so called "zone of insolvency" (i.e., becomes insolvent or is on the verge of insolvency), the duties of the directors shift from those owed to shareholders to one owed to the corporation's other stakeholders. Thus, upon entering the zone of insolvency directors are required to manage and preserve corporate assets for the benefit of the corporation's creditors. Excellent discussions of this issue have been offered in numerous articles during recent years debating the application of a state of insolvency as a component of liability or as a measure of damages.

Many courts apply a "trust fund" doctrine where directors' duties expand beyond the corporate obligations of care and loyalty and also include the duty to deal impartially with the beneficiaries of the insolvent entities assets state. The rationale for this view is that directors of an insolvent entity has [*sic*] special knowledge that is unknown to creditors. Therefore, heightened attention must be paid to avoid conflicts of interest, transactions at less than fair value and potential preferential payments.

Although the temporal and functional parameters of the "zone of insolvency" continue to evolve, it is clear that when an entity is insolvent in fact, directors' obligations and duties will shift to the enterprise as a whole for the benefit of creditors. For purposes of director and officer litigation, solvency is generally determined by evaluating whether an entity is unable to pay its debts as they become due in the ordinary course of business or whether its liabilities exceed the reasonable value of its assets. The time at which an enterprise enters the zone of insolvency is critical because the protections of the business judgment rule may not fully apply, once the entity is in the zone. Demonstrating that directors had knowledge that proposed transactions could render a company insolvent or at the brink of insolvency may be enough to trigger duties owed to creditors. Some courts have indicated that other parties who aided the directors may also share liability for a breach of fiduciary liability owed to creditors of an insolvent corporation.

Transactions undertaken during periods of questionable solvency should be done cautiously this is so due to the intense level of scrutiny such transactions are apt to be subject to after the fact, given (a) the expanded scope of the duties of directors to creditors when an enterprise enters the "zone of insolvency," (b) the continuing ambiguity of the methods for determining solvency and (c) the inherent complexity of asset valuation. It may be assumed that decisions made by directors in real time will be closely scrutinized by creditors after the fact, in order to determine if there were any actionable breaches of the duties owed creditors by the directors.

While operating an entity in or near the "zone of insolvency" directors should take measures showing their exercise of good faith and fair dealing in business transactions. A close examination of decisions in which the courts have allowed creditors to recover for breaches of the fiduciary duties reveals that all such cases involve directors diverting corporate assets for the benefit of insiders or preferred creditors. The most common breaches of director and officer duties to an insolvent entity include: (i) repayment of personal loans or commissions, (ii) payment of loans personally guaranteed by directors or officers, (iii) loss of corporate opportunity; (iv) transactions made for less than fair value for the benefit of related entities, (v) diversion of proceeds or assets resulting in an insolvency, (vi) various forms of self dealing. These types of transactions are always suspect once an entity enters the zone of insolvency and are a red flag for litigious creditors.

To minimize the litigation risk and reduce the potential for director liability with regard to transactions occurring while an entity is in the "zone of insolvency," the directors should engage independent financial advisors to conduct a solvency analysis of the entity, both as it exists before and after a contemplated transaction. This exercise serves at least two important purposes. First, results of the solvency analysis will aid the directors in deciding to whom they owe the fiduciary duties. Second, the analysis will reveal whether a transaction might render an entity insolvent, resulting in increased exposure, after the fact, to lawsuits sounding in legal theories, including fraudulent conveyance, illegal dividend and breach of fiduciary duties to creditors. Third, if a transaction worsens on the financial condition of an entity already in the zone of insolvency, the directors could be subjected to additional claims surrounding in among other things, was and the deepening of the insolvency.

Regardless which test is used in conducting the solvency analysis (i.e., cash flow test or balance sheet test), an entity may be found, in hindsight, to have been insolvent at the time a challenged transaction was consummated, notwithstanding contrary presentations made in the audited financial statements or to the directors.

Conclusion

Mark Twain said he never had to remember anything because he always told the truth. Similarly, directors historically have not worried about what they did, because, if they acted in diligently and in good faith, they were shielded by the business judgment rule. However, recent developments, including both the results of notorious corporate scandals and the adoption of the Sarbanes-Oxley Act, with increased duties to monitor accounting and the relationship between the corporation and its auditors, appear to have increased the showing necessary to establish directors' compliance with the duties of care and loyalty. Elements of this showing may include the adoption

Appendix D: A Primer on Corporate Duties

of an internal audit function and increased scrutiny by the audit committee.

> In the end, unlike Mark Twain, clear indications of reasonable performance should be well documented.

APPENDIX E: ASSURANCE CONUNDRUM

The "Assurance Conundrum" – the challenge to adapt and survive – discusses some of the current challenges facing internal audit from different perspectives.

The aim of this text is to discuss some of the challenges that face our profession at the present time.

Introduction

Having explained the many techniques and approaches that we have, it is now time to provide a brief discussion and explore some of the arguments and ideas that arise in our everyday work.

Board

A view of some board members is that internal audit and risk management are overheads that can be reduced using the same criteria as other costs. As government funding is reduced a popular phrase is "more for less." In defense of this view there is a natural tendency of all internal auditors to highlight the value that successful audits provide to an organization and for risk managers to highlight success in terms of contributions to business plans and strategic direction. Some organizations have explored the options of combined external and internal audit to reduce costs.

However, a question is: can we do more with our internal audit resources? Also, in these uncertain times, what does the Board want more of from internal audit? Internal auditors use international standards and key values, such as independence, but are they enough?

We want assurance of success without the messages that failure is a possibility and, at a strategic level, that errors have not been made for which board members are directly accountable for.

During the recent financial crisis two questions were leveled at risk management: did risk managers ask the right questions and, if so, were they listened to? From an internal audit perspective were we providing assurance on the right issues and, if so, why didn't the Board listen?

This is the key argument for assurance and resources – a reliance on managers with assistance from risk managers to identify the impact of actions and record these in risk registers, and for internal audit to provide assurance that these assumptions are correct and the likelihood has been minimized (internal controls).

Sometimes, in the shadow of risk management is business continuity which is a frequently overlooked function and assurance tool. Some organizations have process improvement functions. New global initiatives, such as environmental sustainability, sold to the Board on the grounds of reduced energy costs may also challenge existing processes and organizational culture.

The key voice to the Board on these issues is the audit committee. For internal auditors, attendance at these meetings can be a pleasure or an unpleasant experience. A necessary evil and, sometimes, an uncompromising and unwelcome obstruction to what we want to do and what we see is important. They act as the bridge between what we

Appendix E: Assurance Conundrum

see as having gone wrong yesterday and what risk management expects to go wrong tomorrow.

In many organizations, to strengthen the messages and warnings to the Board, the audit committee has taken on the governance role, but in many instances it is still seen in isolation and its role not fully understood. This weakness is sometimes compounded by the need for its members to be knowledgeable about the issues and reach a maturity in terms of the overall risk and control framework within the organization. To understand and convey the appropriate message to the Board, does the audit committee need to have control of business continuity and, in the case of public sector organizations, emergency planning?

Does the audit committee have the capacity to become the guardian of any organizations' generic risk exposure? How – with the resources that it has, if all of these tools are available – can it provide the right messages and assurances to the Board and achieve the required response?

One question for internal audit concerns the audit plan. Traditionally, we have looked at specific activities in a particular department and for a particular director without having the need or resources to understand its context and the linkages. Whether we are manufacturing an item or treating a patient there is a clear pathway or experience that crosses many operational boundaries and has many different relationships. To gain our assurance do we audit a number of patients through all of the treatment cycle, or do we cyclically audit specific parts of the pathway? The production manager may want pathway assurance, whilst the finance director may see stock as a specific issue for audit. Both may interpret audits of specific parts of the pathway differently and, therefore, view the value of internal audit in a similar way.

In the public sector, where many organizations are involved in the same pathway, such an audit approach may not be feasible and too complex, but a move towards strategic partnerships is making this action more likely. The key driver in the pathway approach and its attraction to audit committee members is the "reputational risk" of all business relationships.

At the time of writing this article two key events can be used to illustrate this:

- the British Airways' dispute with its contractor, Gate Gourmet
- the massive oil leak problem BP is currently having in the Gulf of Mexico.

In the public sector, where organizations are starting to share locations, a scandal involving one organization can impact on all that are located at the centre and result in a lack of public trust.

In looking at pathways, internal audit can provide independent assurance on the business resilience of the service, challenging managers' assumptions, risk assessments and, more importantly, the impact of changes. In the public sector, managers may look at financial reports and seek to make cuts without understanding the context and impact. A good example of this is home to school transport where demands and, therefore, costs are determined by the number of pupils that are eligible and the location of suitable educational establishments. Financial cuts to the transport budget may not be realistic due to legal responsibilities for learning provision.

Appendix E: Assurance Conundrum

To return to the Board question of: can the internal audit resource do more? Let us re-examine the argument for a secondary role using business continuity. Away from service managers the part of the organization that has the most knowledge of a particular service is internal audit, through its systems, process notes, audit evidence, etc. Surely internal audit is independent! Despite being a non-critical function of an organization, in an emergency resilience should still exist in internal audit functions and it is at this point that the independence issue can be challenged.

Traditionally, internal audit teams work with a lead for a particular client, whether it be a company or a public sector department. To ensure that these relationships continue to be perceived as providing independence, rotation of internal auditors across clients has to take place. Hence, the key contact or the backup can provide the business continuity role. The business continuity role can be used as part of the transition and learning process for the changeover of auditors between clients.

A key part of any internal audit plan is a program or risk-based audit, but what impact has the definition of risk in ISO31000 changed this? The definition of risk in ISO31000 is based on uncertainty. To some risk managers, situations that internal auditors regard as risks are now "issues." So, should this part of the audit plan reflect happened, or certain to happen, events while a separate part of the plan focuses on high impact events, with internal audit providing assurance that likelihood is managed?

Every internal auditor and head of internal audit knows and uses the phrase: "We could provide more assurance if we had more audit days allocated." When a fraud occurs in an area we have not audited, or have audited but with a more limited scope, the defense of audit risk and lack of days appears at a speed faster than "Concorde." When an incident occurs it is not always the manager responsible that is held to account. The manager looks for weaknesses with the information provided, including internal audit reports and risk registers.

To be independent and objective we have to take the view that:

- there is a likelihood that any risk register is out of date and may be incomplete
- due to its organizational profile business continuity plans will be generic and may be out of date, if we don't manage them ourselves
- human tendencies, including managers with careers to pursue and protect, can provide the information that they wish to disclose with plenty of caveats.

Therefore, assessing impact is difficult and likelihood, in the current environments for public and private sectors, is even harder.

The tasks of deciding on the assurance required and providing that level of assurance, without endless resources can seem at times very challenging for audit committees and audit teams delivering the assurance opinions – the "Assurance Conundrum" in its current form.

To conclude these discussion points:

- we have the capability to do more and be valued more
- we have to challenge and support risk management and business continuity more, including via secondary roles

- we have to ensure that our audit committees have the tools and knowledge to communicate our warnings to the Board via thorough reviews of governance processes
- we need to be more challenging of organizational plans, culture and assumptions to ensure the accuracy of our information.

Summary

We live in an ever-changing world where impacts of events are known, but the reality of likelihood varies dramatically. Traditionally, we have looked at what has happened and what might have been. The assurance conundrum, whether you are an internal auditor, a risk manager or a director, is: how can we be assured that uncertainty can be managed? We have the training and the tools, as this book explains, but experienced auditors and risk management academics will tell you the human psyche holds the key. Growth and innovation means taking risks and for all risks there may be no quantifiable controls.

Andrew Dyson

APPENDIX F: THE PERILS OF MOUNT MUST READ™: CONFESSIONS OF A CLIFF NOTE JUNKY[39]

Preface

Why should anyone read a story about a possessed reading pile and a recovering workaholic?

With liberal dose of fantasy and humor, *The Perils of Mount Must Read™* chronicles a quest to conquer the mountain of reading required to just stay competent in information audit and technology.

Admittedly, the intended audience has some background in compliance and IT. Even if the reader is not an IT auditor, the challenge to stay ahead of new tools and research in an industry where "too much information" is a familiar predicament. Add to that, an ego driven compulsion to make sense of every digitally available IT resource, and you have the essence of a modern day tragic hero, an information overload villain, and a quest for information enlightenment. Finding one's life trapped in the race to sustain professional competence is probably not unique to audit or technology.

Blending fiction and truth, the tale aims for insight, suggesting solutions to the problem of what to read and who to regard as "expert" in our field. Laugh with me or at me, but please relax and consider quality over quantity as an alternative to drinking from the digital fire hose.

---

[39] *The Perils of Mount Must Read™: Confessions of a Cliff Note Junky*, Basham R (2006): http://soaprojects.com/flash/The%20Perils%20of%20Mount%20Must%20Read.swf.

Appendix F: The Perils of Mount Must Read™: Confessions of a Cliff Note Junky

Events transpire between October and December, and conclude with the New Year, 2006. Part fantasy and part truth, the characters admit their flaws and evolve a strategy for survival against *The Perils of Mount Must Read*™

Many thanks to the persons who provided a wealth of great resources. Credits are scattered throughout the story and detailed in the endnotes.

Hope you enjoy the read.

Kind regards

Robin Basham, M.IT, M.Ed. CISA, ITsM

APPENDIX G: NORMAN MARKS ON GOVERNANCE

Norman Marks on governance

http://www.theiia.org/blogs/marks/

- What Were the Real Risk and Control Issues at Societe Generale?
- The CAE's Real Challenge - Ethics, Courage, and Complacency
- Risk and Control Issues Commonly Overlooked by Internal Auditing - Part 3
- Risk and Control Issues Commonly Overlooked by Internal Auditing - Part 2
- Risk and Control Issues Commonly Overlooked by Internal Auditing - Part 1

Norman Marks on Governance, Risk Management, and Internal Audit

http://normanmarks.wordpress.com/

- The heart of GRC continues to beat – but what is it?
- The folly of GRC and IT
- Is internal audit irrelevant?
- How does SAP enable world-class GRC processes?
- Auditors and risk models
- The need for information – now!
- Where should internal audit report? Should it be to the audit committee?
- People are the root cause of most risk and control issues

- Why is GRC important?
- Monitoring internal controls and IT
- How do you evaluate your risk management program?
- Are continuous auditing and continuous assurance myths?
- The value of GRC product integration
- Just how effective are risk management practices today?
- Risk-based continuous monitoring/auditing – developments

Norman's shared documents

Norman has uploaded a number of documents to his LinkedIn profile at: *http://www.linkedin.com/in/normanmarks*.

These documents are available for download and sharing and include:

- a paper on continuous risk and control assurance (CRCA)
- the IIA's guide to SOX s404, which Norman wrote
- a copy of an *EDPACS* article by Jay Taylor and Norman Marks on the state of internal auditing
- and more.

APPENDIX H: CHARLES LE GRAND ON TECHNOLOGY

Charles Le Grand is founder and CEO of CHL Global Associates, and a Managing Principal of the TechPar Group. He has more than 30 years' experience dealing with management of security, reliability, auditability, compliance, risk, assurance and governance matters in information and related technologies: *http://chlglobalassociates.com/page2.html*.

Information Technology Controls is co-written by Charles Le Grand, David Richards and Alan S Oliphant. The first *GTAG, Information Technology Controls* covers technology topics, issues and audit concerns, as well as issues surrounding management, security, control, assurance and risk management: *www.theiia.org/guidance/standards-and-guidance/ippf/practice-guides/gtag/gtag1/*.

Information Security Management and Assurance: A Call to Action for Corporate Governance, was co-authored by Thomas R Horton, Charles H Le Grand, William H Murray, Willis DJ Ozier and Donn B Parker: *www.theiia.org/download.cfm?file=22398*.

The Information Security Management and Assurance Series is practical guidance in dealing with information security issues at the Board level and by internal auditors. Prepared by the IIA in cooperation with the US Critical Infrastructure Assurance Office (CIAO), the National Association of Corporate Directors (NACD *www.nacdonline.org*), the American Institute of Certified Public Accountants (AICPA *www.aicpa.org*), ISACA

(*www.isaca.org*) and a host of other supportive
organizations: *www.theiia.org/guidance/technology/it-resources/it-security/*.

The *Software Security Assurance Framework* guide
explains the prevention, detection and correction of security
vulnerabilities in the source code for Internet-facing
systems. This refereed research work contains an executive
summary and management checklist, audit program and
guide, and extensive bibliography:
*www.ouncelabs.com/writable//resources/file/softwaresecuri
tyassuranceframework.pdf*.

Building a Culture of Compliance™ by Charles H Le
Grand, CHL Global Associates, was sponsored by IBS
America, Inc. (*www.ibs-us.com*).

*PC Management Best Practices: A Study of the Total Cost
of Ownership, Risk, Security, and Audit*, co-authored by
Charles Le Grand and Mark Salamasick, was sponsored by
Intel:
*http://www.theiia.org/bookstore/product/pc-management-
best-practices-a-study-of-the-total-cost-of-ownership-risk-
security-and-audit-1141.cfm*.

*Risk Management Approaches to Protection – (Final
Report and Recommendations by the Council)*:
*http://www.dhs.gov/xlibrary/assets/niac/NIAC_RMWG_-
_2-13-06v9_FINAL.pdf*.

ITG RESOURCES

IT Governance Ltd. sources, creates and delivers products and services to meet the real-world, evolving IT governance needs of today's organisations, directors, managers and practitioners. The ITG website (*www.itgovernance.co.uk*) is the international one-stop-shop for corporate and IT governance information, advice, guidance, books, tools, training and consultancy.

www.itgovernance.co.uk/project_governance.aspx is the information page on our website for project governance resources.

www.itgovernance.co.uk/it_audit.aspx is the information page on our website for auditing resources.

Other Websites

Books and tools published by IT Governance Publishing (ITGP) are available from all business booksellers and are also immediately available from the following websites:

www.itgovernance.co.uk/catalog/355 provides information and online purchasing facilities for every currently available book published by ITGP.

www.itgovernanceusa.com is a US$-based website that delivers the full range of IT Governance products to North America, and ships from within the continental US.

www.itgovernanceasia.com provides a selected range of ITGP products specifically for customers in South Asia.

www.27001.com is the IT Governance Ltd. website that deals specifically with information security management, and ships from within the continental US.

Pocket Guides

For full details of the entire range of pocket guides, simply follow the links at: *www.itgovernance.co.uk/publishing.aspx*.

Toolkits

ITG's unique range of toolkits includes the IT Governance Framework Toolkit, which contains all the tools and guidance that you will need in order to develop and implement an appropriate IT governance framework for your organisation. Full details can be found at: *www.itgovernance.co.uk/products/519*.

For a free paper on how to use the proprietary Calder-Moir IT Governance Framework, and for a free trial version of the toolkit, see: *www.itgovernance.co.uk/calder_moir.aspx*.

There is also a wide range of toolkits to simplify implementation of management systems, such as an ISO/IEC 27001 ISMS or a BS25999 BCMS, and these can all be viewed and purchased online at: *www.itgovernance.co.uk/catalog/1*.

Best Practice Reports

ITG's range of Best Practice Reports is now at: *www.itgovernance.co.uk/best-practice-reports.aspx*. These offer you essential, pertinent, expertly researched information on a number of key issues including Web 2.0 and Green IT.

Training and Consultancy

IT Governance also offers training and consultancy services across the entire spectrum of disciplines in the information governance arena. Details of training courses can be accessed at: *www.itgovernance.co.uk/training.aspx* and descriptions of our consultancy services can be found at: *http://www.itgovernance.co.uk/consulting.aspx*. Why not contact us to see how we could help you and your organisation?

Newsletter

IT governance is one of the hottest topics in business today, not least because it is also the fastest moving, so what better way to keep up than by subscribing to ITG's free monthly newsletter *Sentinel*? It provides monthly updates and resources across the whole spectrum of IT governance subject matter, including risk management, information security, ITIL and IT service management, project governance, compliance and so much more. Subscribe for your free copy at: *www.itgovernance.co.uk/newsletter.aspx*.

WHAT OTHERS ARE SAYING ABOUT THIS BOOK

Written with energy, passion, knowledge, and wisdom ... *Raising the Bar* is a handbook for all who strive for excellence, integrity and success in organizations.

Leon A. Kappelman, PhD, Professor of Information Systems and Director Emeritus of the IS Research Center, College of Business, University of North Texas

... here is a cornucopia of riches for the beginning, intermediate, and advanced internal auditor ... the book's approach and tone is always constructive and helpful, and its coverage is quite comprehensive, approaching a trajectory that can only be called encyclopaedic. I heartily recommend this compendium of profound but actionable insights ...

Dr Sridhar Ramamoorti, Associate Professor of Accounting, School of Accountancy, Kennesaw State University

Raising the Bar provides both the big-picture and implementation details for realizing an effective and efficient internal audit function. ... While there are many books on internal auditing, this one rises to the top!

Ron Kral, Managing Partner, Candela Solutions LLC

Raising the Bar opens our mind to infinite possibilities by exposing us to the fundamentals, new ideas, blueprints, guidance, best practices and other tools.

Angelina Chin, CIA, CPA, CBA, CRP, CCSA, Controller General Motors do Brasil

Internal Audit is growing more complex each year. ... This book does an excellent job of providing great resources in one easy to use volume.

Lisa Allnutt, CIA, CISA, Director Internal Audit
Carilion Clinic

If you want to understand the fundamentals as well as the fine points of internal auditing and IT auditing ... read this book.

Eleanor Bloxham, CEO
The Value Alliance and Corporate Governance Alliance

Dan has truly raised the bar for the internal auditing profession and auditing professionals through this knowledge initiative. ... This book can be a true source of knowledge for the internal audit professionals, specifically ... young learners.

Abhik Chaudhuri PMP, ITIL V3f, Cobit Foundation
IBM Accredited Senior IT Specialist

... His thinking is less theoretical and more practical, which makes this book especially important to CIOs, security managers, IT auditors, corporate and IT managers and IT staff responsible for IT infrastructure and systems.

John Kyriazoglou, CICA, MS, BA (Honours)

Through this book, you learn why, what and how to implement proactive risk management controls for greater accountability and fraud deterrence. Dan Swanson has brilliantly hit the mark in assisting small to large companies as well as the public sector with this comprehensive masterpiece.

Anyck Turgeon, Chief of Information Strategy & Security
Crossroads Systems

Lightning Source UK Ltd.
Milton Keynes UK
21 August 2010

158737UK00001B/36/P

9 781849 280679